I always take s]
a high price. Su
So Much More
successful pastors. .....

way that changed everything. The God of miracles invaded this author's life and made life-as-he-knew-it unacceptable. *So Much More!* is the authentic cry from one of this nation's great leaders. He writes with the passion of a prophet and the insight of a disciplined teacher, giving us a road map that directs the reader into a lifestyle of the miraculous through a Christ-like partnership with the Holy Spirit. This book is an outstanding representation of what God is doing in the earth today.

BILL JOHNSON
BETHEL CHURCH, REDDING, CA
AUTHOR, *WHEN HEAVEN INVADES EARTH*
AND *HOSTING THE PRESENCE*

So Much More! Beyond Kingdom Principles to Kingdom Power is a wonderful book about seeking the face of God for your future rather than the facts that surround you. It is fresh and it shows that experiencing Christ, the experience of what we have in the Holy Spirit and in the Kingdom of God, is most important of all. *So Much More!* will warm your heart and cause you to see Jesus above all circumstances and to hear His voice and follow Him according to His Word. Thank you, Todd, for your honesty, directness, and most of all, for your love of the Holy Spirit to be manifested in your life and the lives of others.

DR. MARILYN HICKEY
PRESIDENT AND FOUNDER, MARILYN HICKEY MINISTRIES

Todd Hudson's book *So Much More!* begins with his own journey of discovering the kingdom life, continues with scriptures and personal testimonies that demonstrate the kingdom of God is at war with the kingdom of darkness everyday, and ends with the hope of the fullness of God's kingdom coming to earth when Christ returns. Where many believers would say the gospel of salvation is the ultimate theme of Jesus' ministry, *So Much More!* biblically presents the gospel of the kingdom as the central and quintessential theme of Jesus' ministry, which both encapsulates and places in proper context the gospel of salvation. Solid biblical foundations are laid out in these pages that will open the eyes of the reader to a greater revelation of all the Christian life is purposed by God to be. This is a must read for all Christians who sincerely hunger for more of God in their lives.

JONATHAN WIGGINS
SENIOR PASTOR, RESURRECTION FELLOWSHIP
LOVELAND, CO

Todd's new book gives hope to all those pastors on the journey of moving their church from the Evangelical world to the kingdom-minded church. He tells the story in a way that makes it seem more doable and less scary. Thank you, Todd, for being honest about your feelings and the pitfalls you faced. This book will help many pastors and congregations; they can do this, God is there!

JIM ROGERS
FOUNDER AND DIRECTOR
EXPERIENCING HIS PRESENCE MINISTRIES

SO MUCH MORE

TODD HUDSON

CREATION
HOUSE

So Much More! Beyond Kingdom Principles to Kingdom Power by Todd Hudson
Published by Creation House
A Charisma Media Company
600 Rinehart Road
Lake Mary, Florida 32746
www.charismamedia.com

Unless otherwise noted, all Scripture quotations are from the Holy Bible, New International Version. Copyright © 1973, 1978, 1984, 2010, 2011, International Bible Society. Used by permission.

Scripture quotations marked NKJV are from the New King James Version of the Bible. Copyright © 1979, 1980, 1982 by Thomas Nelson, Inc., publishers. Used by permission.

Scripture quotations marked NAS are from the New American Standard Bible–Updated Edition, Copyright © 1960, 1962, 1963, 1968, 1971, 1972, 1973, 1975, 1977, 1995 by The Lockman Foundation. Used by permission. (www.Lockman.org)

Greek and Hebrew definitions are from Olivetree.com.

Design Director: Bill Johnson
Cover design by: Justin Evans

Visit the author's website: www.kingdomnowministries.org or www.myfreedomfellowship.com

Library of Congress Cataloging-in-Publication Data: 2013952188
International Standard Book Number: 978-1-62136-714-7
E-book International Standard Book Number: 978-1-62136-715-4

While the author has made every effort to provide accurate telephone numbers and Internet addresses at the time of publication, neither the publisher nor the author assumes any responsibility for errors or for changes that occur after publication.

14 15 16 17 18 — 9 8 7 6 5 4 3
Printed in The United States of America

CONTENTS

ACKNOWLEDGMENTS

God has truly blessed me with a godly wife and mother to my children. I love you, Tricia, with all my heart. Thank you for walking every step of this journey with me, being a constant encouragement to get this book done, and serving as my sounding board and informal editor as I tried to put all these thoughts together.

I also want to thank two key friends who have a profound influence on my spiritual journey. Rod Idle is my lifelong friend who has been there for me year in and year out my entire life. It is very rare that God gives us a close friend who is more like a brother. You truly have been the brother I never had! Thank you for writing the forward for this book.

And I also want to acknowledge my good friend Jeff Hutcheon, who was incredibly influential through his teaching and conversations in helping me understand the gospel of the kingdom. I am indebted to you for introducing me to the message and ministry of the kingdom.

FOREWORD

By Pastor Rod Idle

"Something is missing." That sentiment is what I seem to hear often from Christ followers and even pastors about their experience of churches in America. That is how I felt too. I knew there had to be something more. I would look at the picture from the Bible of how the early church operated, but it differed greatly from my personal and pastoral experience.

I read a story once of an Indian chief who came out of his village in the mountains down to the shore of a great ocean. Awed by the scene he asked someone for a quart jar. He bent down and filled the jar with ocean water and sealed the lid. A bystander asked him what he was going to do with the jar of ocean water, and the old Indian chief replied, "Back in the mountains my people have never seen the great water. I am bringing this back so they can see what it is like."

Imagine trying to describe the ocean to someone by carrying a jar of ocean water around. No matter how much we talk about the ocean and carry around a jar full of ocean water, there is no way it could ever be as good as experiencing the ocean firsthand. There is just no substitute for the real thing.

As I read Scripture, I read of healings, demonic deliverance, and even the dead being raised; and I used to wonder, "Why isn't God doing that today?" I would read about it but it only caused me to want it more! So what do we do? Do we just hope for more? Do we just wish for more? In his book *So Much More!* Todd Hudson helps us move beyond the hope of the kingdom of the future to the power of the kingdom today.

More people need to experience what Jesus meant when He talked about the kingdom of God being at hand. We need to understand that He was speaking of the present age as well as heaven. Imagine if Jesus said, "The kingdom of God is at hand...2000 years from now." What power or authority would that bring?

Many good, moral, believing, disciplined, Christ followers operate in a simple hope of living this life the best they can, trying to please the Father, and looking forward to the day when they will be in heaven. As Todd Hudson clearly teaches in this book, the kingdom of heaven Christ came to bring is not just a future event. He speaks of a kingdom that is available to us today that should impact our daily living—a kingdom that is filled with Holy Spirit power that allows us to overcome sickness, demonic presence, and even death itself. It is the life God gives to those born of the Spirit!

I am convinced this kingdom life is what is missing in so many good, God-fearing, truth-teaching, disciple-making churches of today. There is so much more than what we are seeing and experiencing. The Book of Acts and the church of today are meant to be so much more alike than what we have settled for.

God is still victorious. God is still active. God is still able. So why do we settle for the powerless lives that litter our sanctuaries and sometimes even our pulpits?

I did for years. But no more! I will no longer settle for less than what Peter and Paul had. I believe there is Holy Spirit power I can live in today that causes demons to flee, health to be restored, and victory proclaimed! I believe the same Holy Spirit power that Jesus said would allow us to do the things He did and even greater things than even He had done (John 14:12) is available to every born-again believer today just as much as it was available to the born-again believers 2000 years ago!

The partial picture we get through Christ's church today does not do God justice. Christ followers often go through their whole lives without ever seeing and experiencing the power of God. They have seen pictures and heard stories, yet what they hear and what they read in Scripture seems to be very different from their experience. It doesn't have to be that way. There is so much more! Jesus came to restore the kingdom of God, not just point to it. This is much more than something to hope for after we die. It is a hope we have while we live!

I have known Pastor Todd Hudson for over forty years. We are life-long friends. While I have read books in the past about the kingdom age in which we live, it has never been explained so logically and systematically as Todd has done in this book. That, in and of itself, is enough for me. But when you add the sincerity of heart and the authentic faith of a man whom I know so well, it only magnifies the message. Todd's desire is to magnify the message Christ brought to a world that is seeking His truth—a message of hope and power, a message that can change churches and change lives. Are you thinking that something is missing? If you are, then you need to know that there is *So Much More!*

PASTOR ROD IDLE
LEAD PASTOR, JOURNEY COMMUNITY CHURCH
FERNLEY, NV

Chapter 1

MY STORY

WITHOUT ALMOST ANY notice, my life was suddenly turned upside down. One day I was leading as the senior pastor of a conservative evangelical mega church; and the next day I had clearly been led by God to walk away from the security, the financial provision, and the prestige of leading one of the fastest growing churches in our circle of churches in the entire nation and take my life and ministry down a completely different path. People thought I was crazy; but honestly, I was just being obedient to what God called me to do. To understand how I got to that point, I need to help you understand some of my journey.

I have been around church all of my life. I was born into a pastor's family and raised in a very conservative evangelical church. I was called to ministry at a young age; and so to prepare for that I attended a very conservative evangelical Bible college, and shortly after graduating began ministering in churches of that persuasion.

One of the things that I was taught in this background was that God doesn't speak directly to people today, that He usually just speaks through the Bible, or perhaps very occasionally He communicates through an impression He might place on your heart. I was taught that the miracles, signs, and wonders that accompanied believers in the New Testament age were only to give credibility to those establishing the early church; now that the church has been established and we have the Bible in complete form, there was no longer a need for signs, wonders, or miracles. When it came to the Holy Spirit, I was taught much more about what He doesn't do today than what He does do. I learned that He doesn't give people supernatural gifts like tongues, words of knowledge, prophecy, or healing any longer. Again, those gifts had died out and were no longer necessary for today's church. Just like signs and wonders, I was taught that those spiritual gifts were given to add credibility to the apostles' message and help establish the early church; but after the time of the apostles, these things ceased.

Honestly, this teaching never made a lot of sense to me and I was always left wondering deep down inside why my experience in church didn't look more like what I read about in the Book of Acts. However, at the end of the day it did not matter that much to me. What I really wanted more than anything was to see people saved and build a fast growing church.

I was granted success on both fronts. Many people received Jesus as their Savior, and the churches I pastored consistently grew. The first church I pastored was in a small town in Indiana. During the four years I served there, God blessed us with growth from an average attendance of 100 people to about 250. We saw many people receive Christ and be baptized, and it was exciting to watch how God blessed us with growth.

That led to a call from a bigger church in a larger community on the north side of Indianapolis. Again, over the next eight and a half years, God blessed us with growth from an average attendance of 350 people to about 1,000, when I was suddenly and supernaturally called away. My experience of being called away from that church to a new ministry was one of my first encounters with God clearly speaking and leading today in a supernatural and personal way. It seems strange to say, but even after being in church all of my life and having already served for many years as a pastor, I honestly had never experienced God speaking that clearly or leading that supernaturally before.

I loved the church and the community I found myself serving and living in. We had been there for the better part of a decade, and many significant events had happened in our lives during our years there that caused us to become particularly attached to both the people in the church and the community in which we lived. During our years there our family grew, as we welcomed three boys into our family. My mother and father-in-law as well as my wife's two sisters and their families had all moved into the community and were attending our church. My parents were also within a couple of hours, and so our kids had the privilege of seeing their grandparents often. The community and church were filled with young families just like us, and we developed many close friendships. I also had the incredible opportunity to hire my lifelong best friend on our church staff, and we were fulfilling our dream of living in the same community and working together. Additionally, the church was busting at the seams and we were just about ready to put the finishing touches on a brand-new worship center. If you had asked my wife or me, we would have both told you that we were at home in that place and didn't have any desire to move. We saw ourselves raising our children in this community and someday in the future retiring from this church. Life was good and we were enjoying a comfortable ministry, but that was when God stepped in and rocked our world.

In early 2002 I received a phone call from a church in Colorado. Their senior pastor and founder of the church would soon be retiring after leading the church for thirty years, and I had been recommended to them as a potential candidate to take his place. I laughed and told them I wasn't really interested in moving, but they asked if I would at least look at their information and pray about the possibility. I agreed that I would at least do that.

Shortly, I received the material and looked it over. It was a larger church already running about 1,400 in attendance, and the community was one of the fastest growing in the country. It looked like a fantastic opportunity to reach people for Christ and grow a church. But for us to consider moving across the country away from our family, friends, and very comfortable lives, God would have to change our hearts. I prayed a simple prayer, "God, if this is You calling us to this church, then have them keep pursuing me. I won't pursue it because You know my heart and my desire is to stay where I am." Having prayed as I had promised, I confided in my best friend about the opportunity and put the material in a drawer. My wife and I didn't really talk much about it, and I barely gave it another thought.

Three months passed by and I didn't hear anything else from the church. My friend walked in my office one day and asked, "Did you ever send a résumé to that church in Colorado?" I said, "No. I just prayed about it and asked that if this something God is leading in that they would continue to pursue me, but it has been three months and I have not heard another word. I am sure they have moved on to someone else by now; and honestly, I'm relieved because I really want to stay here anyway."

I had barely gotten those words out of my mouth when my assistant buzzed me on the phone to let me know there was a gentleman from Colorado on the phone for me. I recognized his name as being the person who had called me before from the church and I was a little freaked out at the timing, so I told my assistant, "I'm not available right now. Put him into voice mail." I curiously listened to the message later. The voice on the other end said that God had continued to highlight me, and they would really like me to submit a résumé for the position.

I called him back and we talked for a while. I told him I would go ahead and send a résumé but that he need to understand I was not really interested in moving. He said he understood but that they would still like to talk to me. So I sent the résumé and a week later they called back to say they would like to do a phone interview. I told them if they really wanted me to I would agree to the phone interview; however, I again reminded him that I really wasn't interested in moving and didn't want to waste their time. He said, "We understand but we would still like to talk to you."

We did the phone interview and days later they called back asking for a face-to-face interview. They wanted my wife and me to come to Colorado to meet with them. I responded, "I am not sure we should do that because we really aren't interested in moving." Again he assured me they understood but really wanted us to come out and meet with them. Well, at this point I thought it couldn't hurt. We had never been to Colorado before and it might be a fun place to visit if nothing else, and so we agreed to come. The date was set and we would travel to Colorado a few weeks later, which was mid June.

Before we went for that interview, I prayed two things specifically. I asked God if He was, indeed, calling us to move our family across the country and join Him in this ministry, that He would show me two specific signs that weekend of the interview. The first sign I asked for was that I would know that weekend whether or not they believed I was the one God was calling as their new senior pastor. I figured that was a pretty safe prayer, and it really would take a miracle for that to happen. They had, in fact, already told me they had search team members leaving for vacation and would not be able to reconvene to even discuss the interview until after the first part of July so not to be surprised if I didn't hear anything for several weeks following our interview. I also knew this church was already very large and growing rapidly and were replacing their founding pastor who had been there for thirty years. Unless God did something supernatural, there was no way they would make a decision on a new pastor that quickly.

My second sign I asked for in prayer, "God, if this is of You, I want to move my kids before the new school year begins. I don't want to make them move after the school year starts." Again, I thought that was a pretty safe request as it was now only about seven weeks until school would be back in session. Interestingly, we did have a sprinkling of charismatic people within the conservative evangelical church I was pastoring. One of those women, who was an amazing woman of prayer and seemed to hear from God in a way I knew I didn't, came into my office shortly before we were to head to Colorado for the interview. She had no idea any of this was going on, but she proceeded to tell me, "I don't know why, Pastor, but God told me I'm supposed to tell you to read Ezra chapter 1." Knowing her track record of having some right on words from God, I immediately read it while she sat in my office. After I finished reading it I said to her, "I don't know why either. However, that is exactly the place I am at right now in my *Daily Walk* devotional Bible. Maybe there is something in that reading that is for me."

The next morning I got up early to read my Daily Walk devotional Bible. I eagerly turned to the devotion for Ezra chapter 1 wondering if God was going to speak to me. It began with these words: "How long have you lived at your present location? Based on the national average, one family in three will move this year. And that means if you have lived at the place you call home five years or longer you are a vanishing breed."[1] I thought, "Wow! We have lived here for eight and a half years." I read on and the second paragraph talked about a caravan of pioneers in this scripture whom God had lead on a journey of nearly 1,000 miles to accomplish His purpose. I didn't know for sure, but I figured it was probably about 1,000 miles from Indianapolis to Denver. So I quickly looked it up and found it was 1,056 miles.

The last paragraph said, "Is God calling you to pull up stakes, to move to a new home, a new school, a new church, a new job, a new level of commitment to Him? Then here is a motto you may want to copy and display in your home or office: Even a long dangerous journey can be faced confidently when God is leading the expedition."[2]

I quickly went upstairs and woke up my wife. I told her about the woman who came in my office and told me to read Ezra 1. Then I read her the devotional message. She sat straight up and said, "Oh my goodness! We are moving, aren't we?" I told her I didn't know yet. They hadn't even interviewed us, but it sure seemed like God was up to something.

Soon afterward we traveled to Colorado for the interview. We spent all day on a Saturday meeting with the pastoral search team from the church. I did not tell them about the fleece that I had put out to God regarding our weekend together. However, the next morning at church two things happened. Three different members of the search team told me that they had ended up staying after our interview and meeting that night. They proceeded to inform me that the team was unanimous in believing that God was calling me to be their new senior pastor.

Secondly, one of the committee members told me, "I want to make it possible for you to move here before your kids have to start school. I know you have a house in Indiana to sell, and I don't want that to be a burden for you. Find the house here you want and my wife and I will buy it for you. You can live in it until you sell your house in Indiana, and then you can buy the house from us."

My jaw dropped. This could not have been any clearer. I had placed two different fleeces before the Lord in trying to determine His will, and God had very clearly spoken and given me direction. Now I found myself in the incredibly awkward position of having to tell the leaders of my church in Indiana that I believed God was calling us to move when we were within a few weeks of finishing a brand-new worship center. As I shared the story with these godly men, their response was amazing. They encouraged me and told me I must go when God was calling me so clearly. We cried, hugged, and prayed together; and I received their blessing to follow God's call.

I had read many times in Scripture about how God spoke to His people and led them to do specific things, but I had been taught and really believed that God doesn't speak that way today; but I couldn't deny this was the voice of God clearly leading me. This seemed biblical but was completely outside the theology that I had been taught and embraced. In fact, we had people very close to us who told us, "God doesn't really speak like that any more. Those are just coincidences. You just want to move to a bigger church with a bigger salary." But my wife, Tricia, and I knew in our hearts that was not true. God has clearly spoken. However, because of my theological background I still believed this kind of supernatural leading was not the norm but an exception to the rule.

That August we wrapped up our ministry in Indiana. I got to preach in our new worship center one time and then we moved our family to beautiful Colorado. I quickly dove into working hard and facing the challenge of this new, larger ministry with excitement. Again, I was blessed with a church that grew significantly. We saw the attendance explode from an average of 1,400 to about 4,000 over the next few years. We built a new 2,000-seat worship center, and I had a staff that was large enough to allow us to offer many different ministries. It was a fun and exciting season of growth.

I ended up spending about nine years at that church. However, the last few years of that ministry I began to feel a little unsettled and I began to get a sense in my heart that there must be something more. Even through seasons of successful ministries, I found myself questioning why my experience in church wasn't more like what I would read about in the Book of Acts. In Acts, when the Holy Spirit came upon people, they were often guided supernaturally, had dreams and visions of future events, spoke in new tongues, the sick got healed, those oppressed by demons got freed, and on occasion even the dead were raised. My church looked nothing like that. We talked about what Jesus did, and we believed with all of our heart that the Bible was true and the miraculous stories recorded there actually happened; but we had reduced our understanding of the Holy Spirit's role in our lives today to convicting us of sin and leading us into truth.

Then I developed a friendship with a man who was leading a community men's Bible study for the Fellowship of Christian Athletes, and he invited me to attend this study. One of the first series of lessons I attended was about the kingdom of God. My friend taught about how Jesus came to usher in the kingdom of God and how we live in the kingdom today—not some day in the future. He taught that we are empowered by the same Holy Spirit that Jesus was empowered by and that we can do the same works and even greater works than He did. Signs and wonders should follow those who live in the kingdom. This teaching, while new and different than what I had been taught, really resonated with me because it sounded like the church of the New Testament; so I became greatly intrigued. There seemed to be an emptiness in my walk with the Lord, and I began to wonder if this was perhaps what was missing.

A short time later he invited my wife and me to start attending a prayer meeting at his house. We agreed to attend and found there were several charismatic believers in this group. We began to hear people praying in tongues and praying powerfully for things like healing and expecting it to happen! What I noticed most of all was that these people had a passion for the Lord and an expectation for Him to move supernaturally in power that I had never experienced before. They believed the church today should and could look like the church in the Book of Acts. I wanted to know more.

One night at a prayer meeting, one of the men began to pray over Tricia for a new ministry she was beginning. He prayed powerfully in tongues with his hand held up about four inches from her forehead. The next thing I knew, my wife fell down limp. I remember thinking, "Oh my goodness! I think my wife was just slain in the Spirit and she doesn't even believe in that. I know that's not fake!"

Tricia had also come from a very conservative background, perhaps even more conservative than mine. She wasn't at all sure what she thought about these charismatic prayer gatherings, but she was not able to deny that something supernatural had happened to her that night; so she too became intrigued that perhaps there was something more than she had previously experienced.

A couple of weeks later I attended a pastor's meeting at a local charismatic church. I had secretly started building some relationships with people outside my own circle. At this meeting a visiting evangelist prayed over me and I fell down—slain in the Spirit. It was an amazing feeling as I lay there on the ground for several minutes just experiencing the presence of the Lord.

Coming from my conservative background, I obviously wanted to know if being slain in the Spirit was biblical. I talked to one of my charismatic friends who assured me it was. He pointed to Isaiah falling down in the Lord's presence and in Revelation when John was in the Spirit and fell down like a dead man.

All this led me to investigate further about the kingdom, the present role of the Holy Spirit in the life of a believer, and in particular, if signs, wonders, and miracles were still available today through the supernatural work of the Holy Spirit. I remembered a book that someone had told me about probably a decade prior to this by former Dallas Theological Seminary professor Jack Deere called, *Surprised by the Power of the Spirit*. I had never read the book but remembered hearing that it was a story about how God had lead him through biblical study and personal experience to believe the kingdom was here now; that signs, wonders, and miracles still existed today; and that the supernatural gifts of the Spirit were for today. Because of this position he had been fired from the seminary.

I anxiously dove into this book, and as I read his story I was excited to learn that I wasn't alone and that others wondered why our experience in church today was not more like the New Testament church. When I finished this book, I did something I never had done before. I contacted the author. I found out that Jack was preaching at a church in the Dallas area. So I found contact information for the church and I called, I e-mailed, and sent a letter. I thought maybe one of those might get through to him, but I heard nothing. So I kept calling. One day the receptionist at the church told me, "Look, Jack has your information. If he wants to call you, he will." I might be a little dense sometimes, but I got the message loud and clear. I think she was saying something to the effect of, "I am beginning to think you are a stalker. Bug off and leave this man alone!"

A couple of months passed by and I didn't hear anything. I had given up on it and moved on. Then one day my cell phone rang and I answered it. The voice on the other end of the line said, "Todd, this is Jack Deere." I was in shock. He went on to tell me how he was sorry it had taken him so long to reply. He gets many requests from people who read his book and want to meet with him, and he wanted to take some time to pray and see if this was something God was calling him to do before deciding whether or not to reach out to me. He proceeded to invite me to come down and bring my wife and a couple other people if I desired and spend a few days with him.

There were a couple of things that Jack mentioned in that first phone conversation that stuck out in my mind. One was, "Todd, you need to ask yourself if God is changing you or if He is changing your church. Just because He changes you doesn't necessarily mean that He is changing your church." The other was, "I have never seen anyone go down this road as a conservative evangelical beginning to operate in the gifts of the Spirit who has not lost substantial things in their life. You need to decide if you are ready for that."

I was so filled with anticipation about this opportunity to meet Jack and hear firsthand how he had seen the kingdom come and the Holy Spirit do signs, wonders, and miracles today. I decided to take my wife, my friend who taught the kingdom lessons and had invited us to the prayer meetings, and my associate pastor from the church. We all traveled to Dallas and for three days, we sat in Jack's living room. He taught us what the Bible said about the Holy Spirit and how there was clear evidence for the supernatural gifts of the Spirit still existing today. He told us stories about supernatural things he had seen and experienced. He had the opportunity to travel all over the world with John Wimber and see God use them both in supernatural ways to heal the sick, cast out demons, and more. He told us about praying over people and feeling bone grow under his hand. He told us stories about demonic manifestations and the freedom experienced by victims after the trespassers were removed. He had us meet with some of his prophetic team at the church, and they prophesied over us very accurately. I was like a kid in a candy shop, but more importantly I was taken back to the Book of Acts and was so excited that this really was like the church I read about in the Bible! I was ruined. I could not longer settle for anything less.

A short time later I went to men's conference with a local charismatic church. There were about 800 guys there who were on fire for Jesus. The Holy Spirit encountered me that weekend, and what I now believed theologically took place experientially. That weekend I received the baptism in the Holy Spirit; I began to shake and tears streamed down my face and I began to speak in tongues. I had asked for this baptism of fire for a while by this time but nothing experientially had happened. I knew I wasn't going to fake it, but at that conference the Spirit came on me and I was overcome and undone. It was amazing and powerful.

That same weekend I had my first word of knowledge. I heard the Lord say there was a man at this conference who has deafness in one of his ears and the Lord wanted to heal him. I had to leave the conference early but the word was spoken out and a man responded. He said he had deafness in one of his ears. They laid hands on Him and prayed rebuking the deaf spirit and speaking healing and wholeness over his ear. I received an e-mail from one of the leaders a few days later to let me know the man had been healed! A few years later I had the privilege of meeting that man's father and found out he has was still hearing clearly in that ear!

After the trip to Dallas and the men's conference, I was on fire. I went back to the church I was serving and began to teach our leaders what I had been learning. I began to teach our church about the kingdom and the work of the Holy Spirit today. I thought I was going to steer this church of 4,000 people to be hungry for the supernatural;

to see signs, wonders, and miracles; to use all the gifts of the Spirit; and to see the kingdom of God in our church.

I even convinced our church leadership to hire my friend who had taught on the kingdom to help us implement the supernatural gifts of the Spirit into the life of our church. Some of our leaders were excited and ready to go. Others were not so sure but they hesitantly agreed.

One of the first tasks I assigned to this new staff member was to teach our staff about the supernatural gifts of the Spirit and how those gifts were given to us to advance the kingdom in power through signs, wonders, and miracles. We did this as a voluntary lunchtime class. I was shocked that almost every staff member came every week. I was so excited because it seemed as though they were really excited to be learning about the supernatural. The class lasted a few months. Shortly after the class ended, I began to hear some rumblings of disgruntled staff members. So we decided to give the staff the opportunity to give us feedback through an anonymous survey. Given the chance for anonymous feedback, the staff felt safe enough to express their concerns and problems with this teaching. Many of them were completely blown up. They only came to the class because they figured they would lose their jobs if they didn't get on board with the senior pastor's agenda for the church. This was way out of many of their comfort zones and for some even outside their theological beliefs.

After discovering the general feeling of the staff, I decided we needed to slow down. If we were going to turn this big ship, we would have to do so slowly. I backed off of pushing the supernatural work of the Holy Spirit so hard. Some of us who wanted to begin to operate in the gifts and advance the kingdom began doing so behind the scenes as we would meet with people and pray for things like freedom from demonic oppressions and supernatural healing. We experienced demonic manifestations and deliverances. We saw people miraculously healed. But we didn't really push the agenda in the church.

The next spring I went to a School of Healing with Randy Clark and Bill Johnson and I saw God move in amazing ways. I saw a little boy, who had been pulling himself around on crutches all week, walk for the first time in his life. I saw a woman with a severed nerve in her ear hear again. This was actually a creative miracle in which God recreated the nerve in her ear because there was no other way she would have been able to hear again unless that had happened.

I was so fired up after attending that school. Then the next weekend at church I had an amazing personal encounter with Holy Spirit. During one of our church services we were singing Chris Tomlin's song "I Will Follow," and during that song the Holy Spirit came on me and I began to weep. He clearly asked me, "Are you willing to go where I want you to go and do what I want you do?" Then the line in the song that rocked my world was this, "If this life I lose, I will follow You." I knew that the Holy Spirit was asking me, "Even if this life as a mega church pastor with all the perks and benefits and prestige, if you lose all of those things, will you still follow Me?" I said, "I will." That was an amazingly powerful encounter. Holy Spirit spoke to me so clearly.

My response to that encounter initially was to believe I was being called to move forward aggressively in the things of the Spirit and help our church move into the fullness of kingdom ministry accompanied by signs, wonders, and miracles. I knew we needed to implement all the gifts of the Spirit into the life of the church. And I thought that meant I was to push this forward, even if that meant it ultimately resulted in me being fired, because this was the call God that was placing on my life.

A short time later the friend I had brought on staff to help implement the gifts left our staff and our church. That sent me reeling. I had lost the one guy on staff who I knew believed the same way I did and wanted to see the kingdom come in power, so I backed off yet again.

That summer was a rough one for our church. We started experiencing some decline in attendance and offerings. Because of the decline we started the discussion at the leadership level concerning who we might have to lay off. As we were discussing this one day during our leadership meeting, I looked at the team and said, "What about me? Put my name on the list." They said, "Stop joking around like that." I told them I was serious. We had been working on a new vision for the church and no one seemed willing to implement the kingdom and the accompanying power of signs and wonders and miracles into the vision for our future ministry as a church. I told them, "I think maybe it's time for me to move on. I just can't do ministry as usual any more. I know there is so much more!"

Honestly, I shocked even myself to hear those words coming out of my mouth. They told me to go home and talk with Tricia, pray about this decision for a couple of days, and see if I was really serious about this. I went home and told Tricia; her response was, "It's about time. I thought this was going to happen at some point. I know this is what we are supposed to do." Within days I had resigned as the senior pastor of a mega church with no job and no real plan on the horizon, but I had a clear belief that God was calling me on an exciting adventure that would involve so much more than I had ever experienced up to this point.

A month before I resigned, we had invited a local charismatic pastor to speak at our men's conference. I didn't really know him, but I had heard him lead worship and I loved his heart for God. We hit it off the weekend of the conference. Little did I know that a month later I would resign my position. I thought I was going to transition the church into the supernatural gifts of the spirit, not transition me out of the church! But when I resigned God spoke to me clearly and told me this new pastor friend had something to do with my next steps. So I called him and set up an appointment to meet with him. The next day we sat down in his office, and I proceeded to tell him I had resigned from my ministry the night before. He looked at me incredulously and said, "You did what?" So I told him again, and I proceeded to tell more of my personal journey over the past couple of years and how I couldn't do ministry any longer without advancing the kingdom in signs and wonders in miracles and implementing all the supernatural gifts of the Spirit.

He asked me if I had any ideas at to what I would do next. I told him I didn't know but God told me he had something to do with my next steps. He wasn't sure at the moment what that meant, but he agreed he would pray about it. He asked me what I would like to do. I told him that I really love Colorado and would love to stay in the area and plant a church that would bring the kingdom of heaven to earth and move in the power of the Holy Spirit. I explained to my friend that when I resigned I told the leadership of my former church about my desire to plant a church in the area but I also told them I would not do this without their blessing. I didn't want it to look like a church split. I had seen too much of that over the years, and I knew it would do no good to advance the kingdom. It dishonors Christ and His church and I wanted no part of it.

My pastor friend asked me to keep in touch and let me know what the leadership decided. A few days later, I received word that the leadership wanted to bless me to plant a church, but they specified that it could not be in the same town. They didn't want to make it too easy for people to follow me. I called my pastor friend and told him the news. He proceeded to tell me a very interesting story. He explained that God had told him a year prior to this that his church would be involved in a church plant before the end of 2011 (it was now November of 2011) and he had been having his staff prepare for this by writing descriptions of how they would implement their areas of ministry into the life a new church.

This all led to my friend and his church coming alongside us and blessing us as we began planning for this new church. A partnership was formed and they become an integral part of our church plant. They poured into us by allowing us to come and participate in their pastoral staff meetings and build relationships with their staff. They mentored us as to how to develop supernatural ministry into the life of the church. They allowed me to speak at their church and took up a special offering that covered almost all of our start-up costs for the church plant. They also supported the church financially during the initial start-up period. Isn't that just like our God to orchestrate all of these events so perfectly and to provide for us before we ever had the first thought that we would be leaving and planting a new church?

We are now leading a brand-new, kingdom-minded church. We operate in all of the gifts of the Spirit as a church, and we are seeing the Holy Spirit confirm the gospel message with many signs and wonders. We are seeing the Book of Acts come to life and it is life-giving! I am finding out there really is so much more! This journey all began by coming to an understanding of the kingdom.

Chapter 2

THE PRIMARY MESSAGE

As a person who has had an opportunity to teach almost every week, sometimes to thousands of people at a time, I am very concerned about making sure I very clearly communicate the message God has given me. There are certain things that God teaches me through His Word or lays on my heart that are very significant and must be communicated well. When I first was taught how to preach in Bible college, one of the first lessons I learned is that you need to begin with a thesis statement or a big idea that encapsulates in one sentence what you are trying to communicate. Then the rest of the message should simply build upon that by supporting, illustrating, and repeating that central thesis. So when communicating something of significance, the best way to communicate that message is to boil it down to a simple statement, support that statement, illustrate that statement, and repeat that statement, so that when people walk away they know exactly what you were trying to communicate. When this doesn't happen, when the thesis statement is not clearly in place and communicated, there is a tendency to get off track and run down rabbit trails that have nothing to do with the primary message that the speaker is trying to communicate.

Jesus was a master teacher. Teaching was like breathing to Him. He did it wherever He was. He never missed an opportunity for a teaching moment. When we read through the Gospels, we see that He taught on many different ideas and topics, but there was one central thesis to His message that everything else He taught flowed out of. He began His ministry by clearly communicating this primary message and went on to talk about this message more than any other topic.

So what exactly was Jesus' primary message? Let me put it another way; what message did Jesus start His ministry with and what message did He preach about more consistently than anything else? I think many of us would respond by saying it had to be salvation. Surely salvation had to be the first and most consistent message that Jesus taught. Most people, believers and many unbelievers as well, are well acquainted with what is probably the most widely recognized verse from all the Bible; John 3:16: "For God so loved the world that he gave His one and only Son, that whoever believes in him shall not perish but have eternal life." The verse is clearly speaking of salvation and the opportunity to believe in Jesus and receive the gift of eternal life. And I think every Christ follower would agree the message of salvation is indeed a critical message for us to know, believe, respond to, and then proclaim to others; because without a personal belief in the work of Jesus on the cross, there is no salvation. But as significant as we would all agree the message of salvation and receiving eternal life is, it was not the first message Jesus taught and it was not the most consistent message that Jesus taught.

If it wasn't salvation, then what else might it have been? Perhaps some would respond that it was the message of love. One day Jesus was asked, "What is the greatest commandment in the law?" He responded by saying,

"You shall love the LORD your God with all your heart, with all your soul, and with all your mind." This is the first and greatest commandment. And the second is like it: "You shall love your neighbor as yourself." On these two commandments hang all the Law and the Prophets.

—MATTHEW 22:37–40, NKJV

Love God and love your neighbor. Jesus said this was the first and greatest commandment. But as important as this message of love was, we need to ask ourselves if this was the first and most consistent message Jesus taught. Again, there is absolutely no doubt that when you study the teachings of Jesus and you watch the way He lived His life to model for us what a life of love looks like, we see He placed a premium value on love. However, the message of love was not His first message and it was not His most consistent message.

Perhaps some might think that it was the message of the Cross. Jesus called Himself the good Shepherd who came to lay down His life for His sheep. Well, it doesn't take a Bible scholar to know that the Cross was central to the mission of Jesus; but again, it was not the first message and it was not the most consistent message He taught, although it was definitely connected to His primary message.

So if it wasn't salvation, love, or the Cross, what was Jesus' primary message? When the time came for Jesus to begin His ministry, He went to the Jordan River to be baptized by John. He was the Messiah, which literally means in Hebrew "the anointed one." In the Old Testament when kings were set aside to lead the nation, they were anointed with oil as a symbol of being appointed by God for the position. Before Jesus began His public ministry, before He taught anything or performed any miracles, He received His own anointing at the time of His baptism by John.

One day Jesus came to the Jordan River where John was baptizing and He asked John to baptize Him. It must have been an interesting scene to watch. John, knowing who Jesus was, said, "I can't do that. I'm not worthy to even lace your sandals let alone baptize you" (John

1:27). Jesus said, "I need you to baptize me to fulfill all righteousness" (Matt. 3:15). I kind of picture this back and forth tug of war taking place until John finally relented and said, "OK! I will do it!" Then imagine the shocked look that must have appeared on his face and the faces of the crowd when He baptized Jesus and the heavens opened up, the Spirit of God descended on Jesus in bodily form like a dove, and the audible voice of God called out identifying Jesus saying, "This is My beloved Son, in whom I am well pleased" (v. 17, NKJV). That would surely shake up a crowd.

In John 1:33 John states, "I did not know Him, but He who sent me to baptize with water said to me, 'Upon whom you see the Spirit descending, and remaining on Him, this is He who baptizes with the Holy Spirit'" (NKJV). The one upon whom the Spirit descends and remains is the one who will baptize with the Holy Spirit. I picture John out there looking for this One upon whom the Spirit descends and remains. He dunks one—nothing happens. I guess he's not the one. Then another—nothing. Then finally he baptizes Jesus and the Spirit descends and remains on Him and he knows He is the One.

Prior to Jesus, all throughout the Old Testament, there are people upon whom the Holy Spirit descended, but it was always for a specific assignment and was simply a temporary filling. The difference with this filling that Jesus received is that Holy Spirit descended upon Him and *remained upon Him*. And this filling of the Holy Spirit was the anointing that marked the beginning of Jesus' ministry.

Filled with the Holy Spirit, Jesus was led by the Spirit into the wilderness and spent forty days and nights fasting as He prepared Himself to begin His ministry and facing temptation from the enemy to give it all up and take the easy way out (Luke 4:1–11).

When the time of temptation in the wilderness ended with the devil leaving Jesus for a more opportune time, Jesus, anointed by the power of the Holy Spirit, emerged from the wilderness to begin His ministry (vv. 13–14). This first portion of His ministry is often referred to as the Galilean portion of His ministry. As He began His public ministry with preaching and teaching, He began with a proclamation. Out of all of the important subjects Jesus could have chosen to address as He began His ministry, He chose this particular message. And this message He began proclaiming at the beginning of His ministry from that day forward became the most consistent message He taught. In fact, this message would become the overriding theme of everything He taught and everything He did.

What was this central thesis statement of Jesus' ministry that He began His ministry with and proclaimed for than anything else? Mark records the proclamation this way:

> After John was put in prison, Jesus went into Galilee, proclaiming the good news of God. "The time has come," he said. "The kingdom of God has come near. Repent and believe the good news!"
>
> —MARK 1:14–15

So what was the first message Jesus proclaimed? What did He call the message of good news, the gospel message He came to proclaim and is calling us to repent and believe? It was the message of the kingdom. He proclaimed that the kingdom of God is near and that we are to repent and believe this message because this is the gospel message—a message of very good news!

Matthew records that same message with an additional important detail: "From that time on Jesus began to preach, "Repent, for the kingdom of heaven has come near" (Matt. 4:17). From that time on, Jesus preached the same message. That first message became His most consistent message. It was the message of the kingdom; that the kingdom of God was near, at hand, and had arrived on the scene.

In Luke's account he tells us that one of the first things Jesus did after this proclamation was to return to His hometown of Nazareth and go to the Sabbath service at the synagogue. There He made the claim to be the Messiah, the Anointed One, who had come to usher in the kingdom:

> He went to Nazareth, where he had been brought up, and on the Sabbath day he went into the synagogue, as was his custom. He

stood up to read, and the scroll of the prophet Isaiah was handed to him. Unrolling it, he found the place where it is written: "The Spirit of the Lord is on me, because he has anointed me to proclaim good news to the poor. He has sent me to proclaim freedom for the prisoners and recovery of sight for the blind, to set the oppressed free, to proclaim the year of the Lord's favor." Then he rolled up the scroll, gave it back to the attendant and sat down. The eyes of everyone in the synagogue were fastened on him. He began by saying to them, "Today this scripture is fulfilled in your hearing."

—LUKE 4:16–21

In reading this passage from the Old Testament prophet Isaiah (61:1), Jesus was announcing the coming of the kingdom; and in case anyone missed the indirect implication, Jesus made it abundantly clear when He said, "Today this scripture is fulfilled in your hearing." What an amazing statement! Try to imagine yourself in this scene for a moment. You are just going to church for another ordinary Sabbath service and all of a sudden this guy whom you've known all your life, whom you've seen grow up as a young man living in your community and working in His dad's carpenter shop, stands up and reads this Messianic prophecy and says, "I'm the guy who is fulfilling this today in your midst. The time is now. The kingdom is at hand."

The phrase "kingdom of God" appears fifty-three times in the Gospels, almost always from the lips of Jesus. The synonymous phrase, "kingdom of heaven," appears another thirty-two times, primarily in the Gospel of Matthew. This was the first message Jesus proclaimed as He began His ministry, and there was nothing else Jesus talked about more than the message of the kingdom. He declared this to be the gospel. This is the message of good news Jesus came to bring. The kingdom of God has arrived on the scene.

I have to be honest. Even though I had read the New Testament many times, I had somehow missed that this was the primary message Jesus taught. In my first twenty years of ministry, I never preached a message on the kingdom. That is a lot of talking without ever focusing on what Jesus talked about more than anything else. But it wasn't just me. In the conservative evangelical circle I had come out of, I had never heard another pastor do a series of messages on the kingdom. I had never heard another pastor talk about the significance that the good news that Jesus came proclaiming was that the kingdom of God or the kingdom of heaven is near and that He preached that message of the kingdom more consistently than any other message.

Then, as I began my personal journey to understand why the Christian life I was experiencing was not more like what I saw in the Bible, I began to look at the New Testament more closely. And as I studied back through the teaching of the kingdom in the New Testament, I was absolutely astounded at just how central the message of the kingdom was to the life and ministry of Jesus. As I began to pay attention to this, what I found is that the teaching of the kingdom is all over the pages of the New Testament, most of the time from the mouth of Jesus.

Let me give you an overview of what I mean. We see this subject of the kingdom come up even before Jesus came on the scene. In fact, the very same proclamation that Jesus made as He began His ministry first came from the lips of John the Baptist, the prophet sent from God to prepare the way for the coming of Jesus "In those days John the Baptist came, preaching in the wilderness of Judea and saying, "Repent, for the kingdom of heaven has come near" (Matt. 3:1–2). When John arrived on the scene and began to preach, His message was the same message Jesus proclaimed as He started His ministry—repent for the kingdom of heaven is near. Don't miss the significance of this. John was sent by God to announce the coming of Jesus, the Messiah, and the words He used to announce His coming kingdom were, "Repent, for the kingdom of heaven is near."

The Sermon on the Mount recorded in Matthew 5–7 was one of Jesus' most famous sermons. Have you ever noticed how predominant the message of the kingdom was in this sermon? Jesus starts His message with that famous section we call the Beatitudes: "Blessed are the poor in spirit for theirs is the kingdom of heaven" (Matt. 5:3). A little later, in that same sermon, Jesus said, "For I tell you that unless your righteousness surpasses that of the Pharisees and teachers of the law, you will certainly not enter the kingdom of heaven" (v. 20).

It was in this same sermon that Jesus taught His followers how to pray: "This, then, is how you should pray: 'Our Father in heaven, hallowed be your name, your kingdom come, your will be done, on earth as it is in heaven" (6:9).

Again in that same sermon, Jesus talked about how the kingdom of heaven is to be the primary priority of our lives: "But seek first his kingdom and his righteousness, and all these other things will be given to you as well" (v. 33). Over and over again Jesus' message was clear and it was consistent. It was the message of the kingdom.

When Jesus taught, He often told parables—stories to help illustrate a truth. We often refer to parables as earthly stories with a heavenly meaning. The real meaning of the word *parable* is "to come alongside of." Jesus would throw a story along side of a truth to communicate a message. Many of these stories started with the phrase, "The kingdom of heaven is like..." The stories were most consistently told to help us to understand the kingdom.

After Jesus' death, burial, and resurrection, before He ascended back to the Father in heaven, He appeared to the disciples and actually spent forty days instructing them, pouring into their lives. We miss this sometimes. We get this idea somehow that Jesus rose from the dead, appeared immediately to handful of people, and then quickly ascended back to heaven; but that wasn't the case. Now if someone rises from the dead to teach you about something, it's probably worth paying attention to, wouldn't you agree? What did He spend these important last days instructing His disciples about? "After his suffering, he presented himself to them and gave many convincing proofs that he was alive. He appeared to them over a period of forty days and spoke about the kingdom of God" (Acts 1:3).

Not only did Jesus primarily speak about the message of the kingdom, when He sent His twelve apostles out on their first missionary journey, He gave them these instructions: "When Jesus had called the Twelve together, he gave them power and authority to drive out all demons and to cure diseases, and he sent them out to proclaim the kingdom of God and to heal the sick" (Luke 9:1–2). Out of all the messages Jesus could have instructed His disciples to preach, what message did He instruct them to communicate? It was the message of the good news of the kingdom.

A little later Jesus sent not just the twelve apostles but also seventy-two followers on a missionary journey, and He gave them all some very clear instructions about what message to preach: "When you enter a town and are welcomed, eat what is offered to you. Heal the sick who are there and tell them, 'The kingdom of God has come near to you'" (Luke 10:8–9).

Even after Jesus' earthly ministry was completed and the apostles continued His work on earth without His physical presence, yet empowered by His Spirit, we read in the Book of Acts that they preached the message of the kingdom. For instance, Luke, summing up the life and ministry of the apostle Paul, wrote this about him, "He proclaimed the kingdom of God and taught about the Lord Jesus Christ—with all boldness and without hindrance!" (Acts 28:31).

The message of the kingdom was the primary message Jesus preached and was the most consistent message Jesus preached. He charged His apostles to make it their primary message, and they did. I believe the assignment has not changed. We, too, are called to primarily preach the gospel of the kingdom. Much of the church has mixed this up and simply preached a gospel of salvation, that through faith in Jesus you can go to heaven when you die. That's true, but it is an incomplete message. We are not to simply preach the gospel of salvation, but the gospel of the kingdom.

Chapter 3

RESTORING THE KINGDOM

HE MORE I have studied, the more I have become convinced that when Jesus began His ministry with the proclamation "the kingdom of God is near," it was the central thesis statement of His entire ministry. Everything else Jesus taught and everything else Jesus did was simply commentary on what He meant when He said the kingdom of God is near.

In some translations of the Bible the phrase "the kingdom of God is near" reads "the kingdom of God is at hand" (NAS). When Jesus said, "The time has come, the kingdom of God has come near." (Mark 1:15), I believe it is a clear indication that the time had been fulfilled for His kingdom to come and replace another kingdom that was already in place. This is definitely how the Jews in Jesus' day understood it. They had been watching and waiting for centuries for the Messiah to arrive and usher in the kingdom of God here on earth.

So when Jesus arrived and pronounced the kingdom was near, at hand, or arriving on the scene, what was He talking about? Let me explain first what He was not talking about. He was not talking about the church. The church is not the kingdom. The church is people. We are citizens of the kingdom but we are not the kingdom. The kingdom is the rule and reign of God on the earth. That's what Jesus came proclaiming. That is what Jesus came to usher in. Jesus came as God in the flesh and He is the king in this kingdom. His kingdom—His rule and His reign—had come to replace the rule and reign of someone or something else that was already in place. I really should not say He came to introduce the kingdom of God to earth, but actually He came to *reintroduce* the kingdom—the rule and reign—of God to the earth.

The word *kingdom* is made up of two words—*king* and *domain*. When we speak of the kingdom we speak of that which is under the king's domain. The kingdom—the rule, and reign of God on the earth—was here before; but what happened to it and why did Jesus need to come to reintroduce the kingdom? To discover the answer to this question, we must go back to the beginning, back to creation.

Creation starts with God. God is by very definition an eternal being who has no beginning and no end. The very word *God* carries with it the concept of self-existing One or self-sufficient One. God is not a name we simply give to the Almighty One. It is who He is. It is a description of His character. And because He is the only eternal, self-existent, and self-sufficient One with no beginning and no end, He alone qualifies to be given the name "God." God has always existed in this realm that is invisible to us called heaven.

We also know from the Bible that there are angels who live under His authority and serve in His kingdom. At least some of these angels seem to have been delegated a certain amount of authority by God, the King, to use in carrying out His will for His kingdom. For instance, in Daniel's vision recorded in Daniel 12, we learn that Michael is an archangel who serves as Israel's prince. Christian and Jewish scholars alike take this to mean that God assigned Michael the responsibility to be the protector of Daniel's nation, the nation of Israel. God delegated that authority to him. Gabriel, another high-ranking angel, was repeatedly called upon to communicate messages from the King to mankind. For instance, Gabriel was sent to announce to Daniel a message about the end of days (Dan. 9:27–27), and in the New Testament we find him being sent by God to announce the births of both John the Baptist Luke 1:11–21) and Jesus (vv. 26–37). He was given authority and responsibility by the King.

Then there was the angel named Lucifer. He was also one of the archangels. Some speculate that he might have been the highest ranked archangel of all. Scripture seems to indicate that he was given authority over worship. He was the worship leader in heaven in eternity past. One day, he became consumed with pride and began to think, "I should be the king of this kingdom." He convinced some of the angels to join him as he led a rebellion against the King, God. Of course, he was unsuccessful in his rebellion, and the Bible tells us that he was kicked out of heaven along with a third of the angels who had joined him in this rebellion. (See Isaiah 14:12–14; Ezekiel 28:12–17; Luke 10:18; Revelation 12:3–9.) He then went about setting up his own kingdom. As we read Scripture, it seems to indicate that God allowed Lucifer, this fallen angel we know as Satan, to retain at least some of his power and he utilized this to develop and advance his own kingdom.

At some point after this fall, God expanded His kingdom by creating a new visible kingdom called earth. He culminated His creation with the masterpiece of all of His creation, human beings, made in His very own image. God created Adam and then Eve and He placed them in this beautiful place, the ultimate expression of His beauty and peace, called the Garden of Eden. When the King, God, created Adam and Eve and placed them in this new visible kingdom called earth, He gave them a commission. We read about this in Genesis 1, and this section is absolutely foundational if we are ever going to understand the idea of the kingdom that Jesus came to reintroduce to the earth.

> Then God said, "Let us make mankind in our image, in our like-
> ness, so that they may rule over the fish of the sea and the birds
> in the sky, over the livestock, and all the wild animals, and over
> all the creatures that move along the ground." So God created
> mankind in his own image, in the image of God he created them;
> male and female he created them. God blessed them and said
> to them, "Be fruitful and increase in number; fill the earth and
> subdue it. Rule over the fish of the sea and the birds in the sky
> and over every living creature that moves on the ground."
> —Genesis 1:26–28

When God created Adam and then Eve, He stated His purpose for them in this world. It was not just for them individually, but this was God's purpose and intent for all of mankind. In verse 26 before He created man, God stated this purpose, "Let us make man in our image and let them rule over the fish of the sea, the birds of the air, the livestock and over all the earth." Then after God created mankind, He stated this purpose directly; basically saying, "I want you to subdue the earth and rule over it." Some translations use the phrase "take dominion." Dominion speaks of the rulership of a king over a kingdom. The definition of *dominion* can be stated this way: "To be given dominion means to be established as a sovereign, kingly ruler, master, governor, responsible for reigning over a designated territory, with the inherent authority to represent and embody as a symbol, the territory, resources and that constitutes a kingdom."[1]

When God gave mankind dominion on the earth, what did that mean? God was delegating to mankind the authority to rule and reign on the earth on behalf of the King of this universe. There was a divine transfer of power and authority that occurred. This is very important for us to understand if we are going to get our arms around God's original intent and purpose for mankind.

So at this point, Adam and Eve were created by God and placed in this new visible kingdom called earth. The kingdom of heaven and the kingdom of earth were one, and God delegated the authority to Adam and Eve to take dominion, to rule and reign in this extension of His kingdom on His behalf.

This new kingdom was one with the kingdom of heaven, and it was like heaven on earth. There was no disease, pain, or death. It was a perfect kingdom, God's kingdom; and it was God's intention for mankind to live in this perfect kingdom and take dominion over the earth. Originally, the kingdom of heaven and the kingdom of earth were one with God as the King; but God, the King, said to Adam, "I am delegating to you the responsibility to take dominion, to rule over the earth on My behalf."

After Satan's rebellion against God, instead of destroying him, God banished him from heaven. Jesus said, "I saw Satan fall like lightning from heaven" (Luke 10:18). When Satan was banished from heaven, he began to work to establish his own kingdom. The problem he faced was that he had no domain, no place to take authority. He was looking for a kingdom to call his own. When Satan came to the garden that day to tempt Adam and Eve, he came looking for dominion. He came to entice Adam and Eve to rebel against God's kingdom and thereby transfer to him the authority that God had delegated to them.

Satan came in the form of a serpent and convinced Adam and Eve that if they ate the fruit that God said not to eat, they would become like God. In other words, they would no longer have to rule underneath God's authority, in His kingdom, but rather they could have their own kingdom. Foolishly, Eve and then Adam agreed to doubt God, to rebel against and disobey their King, God; and in the process they became obedient to Satan. (See Genesis 3.) In obeying Lucifer, Adam and Eve gave away the dominion that God had given to mankind to rule and reign on the earth. All that was under Adam's authority fell when Adam fell. His disobedience brought a curse on all creation and allowed Satan to usurp the authority that God had delegated to Adam and Eve and he took dominion over this world. Because of Adam and Eve's fall, this world became Satan's domain. The Bible tells us repeatedly that he has usurped dominion and become the ruler of this world. Jesus referred to Satan as "the prince of this world" (John 12:31).

Satan is referred to by Paul as "the god of this age" (2 Cor. 4:4), and as "the ruler of the kingdom of the air" (Eph. 2:2).

We even see Satan's dominion over earth in the temptations of Jesus.

> The devil led him up to a high place and showed him in an instant all the kingdoms of the world. And he said to him, "I will give you all their authority and splendor, for it has been given to me, and I can give it to anyone I want to. If you worship me, it will all be yours."
>
> —LUKE 4:5–7

When Jesus responded, He said He refused to bow and worship anyone but God (v. 8), but He did not challenge Satan's claim that the kingdoms of the world were his to give away.

So when Adam and Eve sinned, Satan usurped the dominion given to mankind. Notice that Satan didn't come into the garden and forcefully take away the kingdom from Adam and Eve. He couldn't do that. He had no dominion there. Dominion empowers; and since the King, God, had delegated this authority to mankind, the only way that Satan could get the dominion he desired was for mankind to give it to him. So the suggestion to eat the forbidden fruit was Satan's attempt to get mankind to agree with him in his rebellion against God and transfer that authority that God had given to mankind to rule and reign in this world over to Satan—and it worked. God had given dominion over the earth to Adam; but when he chose to sin, he also chose to hand over that dominion to Satan. It was the greatest act of treason that has ever been committed. In that moment when Adam and Eve rebelled against God and chose to sin, mankind became a slave to a new king. All that Adam and Eve had been given, including the title deed to this planet and the delegated authority to take dominion and rule over the earth on behalf of the king, was handed over to Satan. And all of a sudden mankind was no longer living in the kingdom of God, enjoying the dominion God had delegated to them to rule and reign on the earth; but now they found themselves living in Satan's kingdom, under his rule and reign. The result was pain, sickness, suffering, and death—all those things that represent that the kingdom of darkness now had dominion on planet earth. And the earth that mankind was created to take dominion over was now cursed and his authority was stripped away.

This is really important for us to understand. If we don't understand that the kingdom was lost, that initially there was a position of authority given to mankind to take dominion over the earth that was usurped by Satan, then we won't understand the importance of Jesus coming and proclaiming that the kingdom of God is at hand. Because in that declaration He was stating that He had come to take back the kingdom. He came as the second Adam, to take back the kingdom and reestablish the rule and reign of God on the earth. He came to defeat the kingdom of Satan and render it powerless. He came to make it possible for mankind to move back into the position God intended for us to have in the first place—to live in God's kingdom and rule and reign with Him by taking dominion over the earth.

"For this purpose the Son of God was manifested, that He might destroy the works of the devil" (1 John 3:8, NKJV). This is why Jesus came. He came to destroy, render powerless, the kingdom of Satan and reintroduce the rule and reign of God to the earth and give mankind back the dominion that had been delegated to him by God before the fall. That is why the kingdom was the first message Jesus proclaimed, and that is why this was the most consistent message He proclaimed.

When Jesus came proclaiming this message of the kingdom, He was clearly throwing down a gauntlet in the face of Satan. It was a declaration of war, because He came to take back the dominion that Satan had usurped over the earth when mankind sinned; and this is exactly how Satan perceived Jesus' coming. There is no mistaking the fact that Satan knew exactly who Jesus was and he knew why He had come.

In Mark 1, shortly after Jesus' proclamation that the kingdom was at hand, Jesus went to preach in Capernaum in the synagogue and a demon manifested in a man attending the church service that day and called Jesus out.

> Just then a man in their synagogue who was possessed by an impure spirit cried out, "What do you want with us, Jesus of Nazareth? Have you come to destroy us? I know who you are—the Holy One of God!"
>
> —MARK 1:23–24

That demon knew more than anyone else in the synagogue that day about who Jesus was and why He had come. That is why demons often shrieked in the presence of Jesus and they asked questions like we see in this passage, "Have you come to destroy us?" They knew this was war. The demons trembled with fear at the message of the kingdom. They knew why Jesus had come. He came to reestablish and say in effect to Satan and his demonic forces, "Your kingdom is coming to an end. It is going to be rendered powerless."

If Jesus came to reestablish God's kingdom on earth and to give mankind back the dominion we lost in the garden and to erase Satan's power and authority of sickness, pain, and death, then why are we still experiencing those things? Was He really ushering in the kingdom of God—the rule and reign of God—now? Or was He merely talking about the kingdom—the rule and reign of God—arriving at some later time in the future?

In some of Jesus' teaching He appears to say that the kingdom of God is a future realm that will come some day when He returns to earth. For example, at the Last Supper when Jesus introduced the cup of remembrance and told His disciples to drink this in remembrance of Him, He also said, "I tell you, I will not drink this fruit of the vine from now on until that day when I drink it new with you in my Father's kingdom" (Matt. 26:29). It seems that He was speaking of the kingdom as being a future reality, or in other words, the millennial kingdom.

Peter wrote,

> Therefore, my brothers and sisters, make every effort to con-
> firm your calling and election. For if you do these things, you
> will never stumble, and you will receive a rich welcome into the
> eternal kingdom of our Lord and Savior Jesus Christ.
>
> —2 PETER 1:10–11

Peter is clearly speaking of a future day when we will enter His
eternal kingdom. Another example is found in Matthew 25. Jesus is
speaking of the final judgment day when He says,

> Then the King will say to those on his right, 'Come, you who are
> blessed by my Father; take your inheritance, the kingdom pre-
> pared for you since the creation of the world.
>
> —MATTHEW 25:34

Obviously, this passage is speaking of the kingdom in terms of the
future. This is how many people have viewed Jesus' entire teaching
about the kingdom. We have in large part ignored this message that
Jesus proclaimed first and most consistently because we have dismissed this message as having nothing to do with the here and now
but simply being about a kingdom that will come at some point in the
future.

I believe that one of the reasons this message of the kingdom has
been primarily ignored by the church is that we think what we are
supposed to do is get people saved so they are ready for the kingdom
some day. We mistakenly think the kingdom has nothing to do with
life here and now. If Jesus had only spoken of the kingdom in a future
tense, that would make sense. But as we study the teaching of Jesus,
we learn that He not only spoke of the kingdom in a future tense, He
also spoke of the kingdom being a present reality as well. We see it
in this very proclamation He made as He began His ministry, "The
kingdom of God is near, it is at hand." He came to reintroduce that

which was lost, to reestablish the rule and reign of God on the earth and restore dominion to mankind today—not just in the future.

Matthew 11:12 says, "From the days of John the Baptist until now, the kingdom of heaven has been subjected to violence, and violent people have been raiding it." When He spoke those words, He indicated that the kingdom of heaven had already been reintroduced to earth and had already begun advancing. In this passage He is speaking of the kingdom as a present reality, not a future event.

One day Jesus was asked by the Pharisees when the kingdom of God was coming, and He answered, "The coming of the kingdom of God is not something that can be observed, nor will people say, 'Here it is,' or 'There it is,' because the kingdom of God is in your midst" (Luke 17:20–21). Jesus is very clearly saying that the kingdom is here now today and we are not to simply wait for a kingdom to come in the future. We live in the kingdom today.

Another clear example of how Jesus demonstrated that the kingdom was here now is found in Matthew 12. The religious leaders had accused Jesus of driving out demons by the power of Beelzebub, or Satan. Jesus said basically, "Why would Satan drive out Satan? A house divided against itself cannot stand" (Matt. 12:25–26). Then He pointed to the true source of His power and authority over the enemy, the Spirit of God, when He said, "But if it is by the Spirit of God that I cast out demons, then the kingdom of God has come upon you" (v. 28). Jesus pointed out that the reason He was able to take authority over the enemy by telling demons what to do and they obeyed Him was an indication that the kingdom of God was already present.

The kingdom of God is a present reality demonstrated by the authority Jesus took over the kingdom of Satan. But we also see that there is coming a future kingdom, the millennial kingdom, when Christ will rule on this earth and the kingdom of Satan will be completely destroyed. So which is it? Is the kingdom now or not yet? And the answer is yes! It is both now and not yet.

When Jesus started His ministry by proclaiming the kingdom of God is at hand, He was in essence saying, "It is here now. I have come to usher in the rule and reign of God today among you." But while Jesus reestablished the rule of God on earth in the present, the realm of God's reign over the entire earth will not be reestablished until the Messianic kingdom when King Jesus reigns on the throne and Satan is bound.

Dr. George Eldon Ladd titled one of his books about the kingdom *The Presence of the Future.*[2] He was communicating the concept that the kingdom is both a present reality and something that will come in fullness at some point in the future. The future is coming toward us, it isn't completely here, and yet it's partially here. But because Jesus came to reestablish this authority of God on the earth, to give us back the dominion we lost in the garden, we can choose to live under God's rule and reign now, today! We have the opportunity today to come out from under the darkness of the enemy who has come to steal, kill, and destroy (John 10:10), and move into God's kingdom, a kingdom of light, a kingdom of freedom, and kingdom of power in which the King has restored to us dominion over those things that the enemy wants to use to keep us in bondage.

Chapter 4

CLASH OF KINGDOMS

J ESUS CAME WITH both a message and a ministry. What was His primary message? The kingdom of God is at hand. What was His primary ministry? The kingdom of God is at hand. The message Jesus spoke about the kingdom cannot be separated from the works Jesus did that demonstrated the kingdom. Jesus came proclaiming the truth that the kingdom of God was at hand and that was the illumination of His mission in the world; but the works Jesus did were the illustration that the kingdom of God had come to invade the dark kingdom of the enemy who was ruling and reigning in the world. Everything He did was carefully designed to prove this message that He preached about the kingdom.

I think much of the church today has missed this connection between the words of the kingdom and the works of the kingdom.

Many have noticed that Jesus talked a lot about the kingdom, but most seem to ignore the connection between the words about the kingdom and the works He did that demonstrated He had come to usher in the kingdom today. Thus, instead of recognizing that we live in the kingdom today and must preach both the message of the kingdom and do the ministry of the kingdom, many have simply assigned the message of the kingdom to future events, such as when we got to heaven or when Jesus returns to rule and reign on the earth in the millennial kingdom. However, when we recognize that Jesus didn't just preach a message about the kingdom but His ministry demonstrated that the kingdom of God had invaded the kingdom of this dark world today and He took dominion over the works of the enemy today, it will change everything about how we do ministry.

When Jesus healed the sick, took authority over demons, multiplied the five loaves and two fish to make it a meal capable of feeding 5,000 men plus women and children, turned water into wine, or raised the dead, all of these things were carefully calculated to demonstrate and validate the message that He had come to usher in the kingdom. The Bible says that Jesus came to destroy the works of the devil (1 John 3:8) and every time He took authority over the works of the devil it was a demonstration of the truth that He had come to reintroduce the kingdom—the rule and reign of God on earth.

One of the most freeing things that Jesus did that demonstrated that the kingdom of God had invaded earth to bring an end to Satan's kingdom and replace it with the rule and reign of God, was that Jesus delivered people from demons who were polluting, contaminating, disrupting, and destroying their lives. These demons had been victimizing people, wreaking havoc, and attempting to destroy their lives; and Jesus set these people free! Every time Jesus took authority over demons, it was a clear demonstration of the message of the kingdom. He had come to confront and bring an end to Satan's rule and reign on the earth.

For most of my ministry, when I would read in Scripture of Jesus casting out a demon, I didn't really relate that to me or to my ministry today. I had never had an encounter with a demon. I had been taught that there really weren't people who had demons that needed dealt with today, except maybe in some of the dark third world countries, so I thought I was pretty safe from encountering demons in places like Indiana and Colorado. However, after several encounters where I have seen demons manifest and I have taken authority over these demons and seen people set free, I have come to recognize that demons are real and are still tormenting people today, even in America. It is an amazingly beautiful thing to see the gratitude and the freedom people experience when demons that have been trespassing in their lives are removed. Some of them have been tormented and victimized from early childhood by these demons that had come upon them to oppress them, bring pain to their lives, and to destroy them. Sometimes the effects are physical, sometimes emotional, sometimes social, or at times even all three, depending on the demons working in their lives. But the good news of the kingdom is that Jesus came to destroy the works of the devil. And throughout Jesus' ministry one of the kindest things He did for people was set them free from demonic oppression; and in doing so, it was a clear demonstration that the kingdom of God had come to replace the Satan's rule and reign on earth.

In Mark 1 there is a story that takes place immediately after Jesus' baptism in water and the filling of the Holy Spirit and that initial proclamation He made that the kingdom of God is near. Jesus went to the local church, the synagogue, and stood up and began to read Scripture and teach. This is the first public teaching of Jesus' ministry that we have recorded in the Bible: "They went to Capernaum, and when the Sabbath came, Jesus went into the synagogue and began to teach" (Mark 1:21). We don't know for sure what message Jesus was teaching that day because it doesn't specifically tell us in the text, but I have a feeling it was this same message that He had just proclaimed as He started His ministry and the message that Matthew said He preached from that day forward. It was likely the message of the kingdom. It was the message that proclaimed, "The kingdom of God is near. Repent and believe the good news!" (v. 15). As you dig down into the Gospels and the messages Jesus taught, the kingdom was the topic He almost always taught about.

When the people heard this teaching, it says, "The people were amazed at his teaching, because he taught them as one who had authority, not as the teachers of the law" (v. 22). Notice, there was a difference between Jesus' teaching and the teaching the people were used to. The difference is in the area of authority. Jesus had a different level of authority in His teaching that the people had not experienced before because He was preaching that He had come to reestablish the kingdom.

> Just then a man in their synagogue who was possessed by an impure spirit cried out, "What do you want with us, Jesus of Nazareth? Have you come to destroy us? I know who you are—the Holy One of God!" "Be quiet!" said Jesus sternly. "Come out of him!" The impure spirit shook the man violently and came out of him with a shriek. The people were all so amazed that they asked each other, "What is this? A new teaching—and with authority! He even gives orders to impure spirits and they obey him." News about him spread quickly over the whole region of Galilee.
>
> —MARK 1:23–28

This was the initial confrontation between the kingdom of God and the kingdom of Satan during the time of Jesus' ministry. It was a declaration of war that clearly illustrated that Jesus had come to usher in the kingdom of God and replace the rule and reign of the kingdom of Satan.

This whole scene took place in the synagogue, at a church service, if you will. I doubt if you have ever been to a church service like this one before. If you have been, it is one you would never forget. It started out much like any other Sabbath day. The people had gathered at the synagogue to worship and pray; and then this guy, Jesus, stood up and began to read the Scripture and teach. As He taught, the people began to notice that His message was different. There was a new power and authority in the way this guy taught far beyond what they had experienced when they listened to their own rabbis teach from Scripture. Then, as Jesus was teaching, right in the middle of this church service, a man stood up and started screaming at Him. That is not your ordinary church service! This man started screaming; but what we see is that it was not really the man who was screaming, but demons that are trespassing in this man's body are using his voice to shout at Jesus: "What do you want with us, Jesus of Nazareth? Have you come to destroy us? I know who you are—the Holy One of God!" (v. 24).

There is absolutely no confusion at all in the minds of the demons as to who Jesus is. They clearly point out that He is Jesus who hails from Nazareth. Everyone else in the room perhaps would have known this as well, but the demons also refer to Him as the Holy One of God, which was something no one else in the room would have been capable of knowing. The demons knew more than anyone else present that day about who Jesus really was. Not only did they know who He was, they knew why He had come. They asked, "Have you come to destroy us?" That really was kind of a rhetorical question. They knew that He was the Holy One of God, whom they had lived with in heaven in eternity past and had known as the Lord of heaven, the Eternal One who existed before the foundations of the world. They also knew that His coming and invading their territory was not a good thing for their kingdom. These demons knew exactly who Jesus was and what He had come to do. They were screaming at the top of their lungs, "Have you come to destroy us?" The answer to their question was yes. He had come to destroy their dominion take back the kingdom. He had come to put an end to their rule and reign. He had come to destroy the works of the devil.

This group of demons were trespassing and victimizing this poor man, and Jesus had come to bring deliverance to him. It was going to be one of the most beautiful, loving, and freeing things this man would ever experience in his life. This man would never be the same the rest of his life because Jesus showed up and delivered him from demons that had been tormenting him. The scripture here says in some translations that this man was "possessed." That is not the best choice of words because it implies ownership, and that may not necessarily be the case. If we go back to the original language, the word "possessed" does not appear. The Greek word translated "possessed" is actually the word *daimonízomai*, which literally means to have a devil, to be exercised by an unclean spirit, to be under the power or influence of one, or to be vexed with a devil.[1] To be vexed refers to harassment, torment, and troubling from an evil spirit. Many scholars believe a better translation of the word would be the word "demonized" rather than "possessed," and that would be an important distinction.

Much of the modern language we use to describe demonic activity in the lives of humans is not helpful or biblical. For example, we sometimes debate whether or not Christians can be demonized. Can demons be in, at, or around believers? Nowhere does the Bible tell us that Christians cannot be demonized or have some level of demonic activity coming against them. The most commonly used argument for saying a believer cannot be demonized is a theological argument rather than a biblical argument. The question is usually asked this way: How can Christ and a demon dwell in the same home? The answer to this question might be stated in the form of another question: How can Christ and sin dwell together in the life of a believer? The fact is the Holy Spirit dwells with sin any time He inhabits the heart of a believer. If He can dwell in the heart of a sinful person, could He not dwell with a demonized person?

Let me just mention one example from Scripture that indicates that Christians can be demonized at some level.

> It is actually reported that there is sexual immorality among you, and of a kind that even pagans do not tolerate: A man is sleeping with his father's wife. And you are proud! Shouldn't you rather have gone into mourning and have put out of your fellowship the man who has been doing this? For my part, even though I am not physically present, I am with you in spirit. As one who is present with you in this way, I have already passed judgment in

the name of our Lord Jesus on the one who has been doing this.
So when you are assembled and I am with you in spirit, and the
power of our Lord Jesus is present, hand this man over to Satan,
for the destruction of the flesh, so that his spirit may be saved on
the day of the Lord.

—1 Corinthians 5:1–5

This seems to indicate that sexual sin, including lust, immorality, adultery, and perversion, can open up a door for demonic activity in the life of a believer. Notice Paul instructs that this man be handed over to Satan. Yet he is a believer, a member of the church, and his spirit is going to be saved on the day of the Lord.

There are also several scriptures that warn us as believers against activities that can give demons inroads into our lives. One example: "'In your anger do not sin.' Do not let the sun go down while you are still angry, and do not give the devil a foothold" (Eph. 4:26–27). When we carry around unresolved anger and unforgiveness in our hearts, Paul says we open a door for demonic activity in our lives.

The Bible also says that things such as hatred, violence, envy, jealousy, selfish ambition, occult practices, idolatry, and blasphemy can create demonic inroads into the life of a person, even a believer. So we should not be naïve enough to believe that simply because we are believers we are immune from opening a door to the enemy and allowing him access to our lives. Peter was writing to Christians when he said, "Be alert and of sober mind. Your enemy the devil prowls around like a roaring lion looking for someone to devour" (1 Pet. 5:8). I think it is pretty clear that Christians can be demonized at some level.

The man who encountered Jesus in the synagogue in Mark 1 was clearly demonized. The demons were abusing this man and causing him harm. When Jesus saw that, He was filled with compassion and mercy for the man and wanted him to be free. So He spoke to the demons and took authority by rebuking them and telling them to be quiet (1:25). The English translation doesn't do the Greek language justice here. The word Jesus used was powerful. The Greek word translated "be quiet" means to muzzle or put to silence, and the word translated "come out" means to go or depart. When you put these together, it might be translated "Stop it!" He was rebuking the demons and demanding that they stop oppressing this man and leave him alone. The clear implication was that they didn't really have a choice. They knew who Jesus was and they had to listen to Him because He had authority over them. Then Jesus demanded that the evil spirits come out of this man. The evil spirits shook the man violently and came out of him with a shriek. It was all over in a matter of seconds from the time Jesus spoke until the man was freed from this demonization. Jesus was not an exorcist. Jesus was a demon-expeller. He had the power and authority to drive demons out with a word, and in doing so He is demonstrating for us that the kingdom of God is here.

Notice the reaction of the people. They knew about exorcism. The rabbis of Jesus' day practiced a type of exorcism. They would recite the sacred name of Yahweh, and they had some success in causing demons to leave. Historians of the day speak of those who practiced rituals, incantations, and spells using things like potions, herbs, rings, or other objects that were thought to have magical qualities to cast out demons. However, all of these things took time and had limited success in exorcising demons.

But there was something different about Jesus. There were no incantations or spells. He spoke orders and demons obeyed. He did it with a word—a command. What we are seeing here is kingdom power. The people recognized the authority Jesus operated under was unique. They had never seen anyone with this kind of authority. In an instant, the secret activity of the enemy was exposed and halted, and Jesus did it all with just a word. In this instance, the demon threw the victim to the ground, shrieked, and left within simply a matter of seconds. It happened instantly, and the people who saw this were astonished. They had never seen anyone operate in this kind of authority before. They had never witnessed anyone with the power and authority to give orders to demons before, and what was even more amazing was that the demons obeyed! They were witnessing Jesus in all His power and authority.

There is another passage that makes this connection between Jesus taking authority over demons and the reintroduction of the kingdom of God.

> Then they brought him a demon-possessed man who was blind and mute, and Jesus healed him, so that he could both talk and see. All the people were astonished and said, "Could this be the Son of David?" But when the Pharisees heard this, they said, "It is only by Beelzebub, the prince of demons, that this fellow drives out demons." Jesus knew their thoughts and said to them, "Every kingdom divided against itself will be ruined, and every city or household divided against itself will not stand. If Satan drives out Satan, he is divided against himself. How then can his kingdom stand? And if I drive out demons by Beelzebub, by whom do your people drive them out? So then, they will be your judges. But if it is by the Spirit of God that I drive out demons, then the kingdom of God has come upon you.
>
> —MATTHEW 12:22–28

The religious leaders accused Jesus of driving out demons by demonic power. They said He was working on behalf of Satan's kingdom. Jesus responded by saying, in effect, "Let's just think this through rationally. Whether we're talking about a kingdom, a city, or a household, if it is divided against itself it will not stand." Jesus is saying it doesn't make sense to think that He would drive out Satan himself by Satan's power. What was really going on was a clash of kingdoms. Jesus had come to usher in the kingdom of God and take on the kingdom of Satan, and His authority over demons was proof that this kingdom had come.

This same power has been delegated to us as believers today. Following Jesus' death, burial, and resurrection, the enemy was fully and finally defeated. Jesus stood in front of His disciples and declared, "All power and authority in heaven and on earth has been given to me" (Matt. 28:18). The implication was that all the power and authority that had been usurped by the enemy in the garden had been taken back by Jesus. Then He told His disciples to go and do what He had been doing. In other words, "I got back all power and authority. It has been given to Me, and I am conferring this power and authority to you." He wanted them to go fulfill their original assignment—to live in the kingdom of light and take dominion over the earth and destroy the works of the enemy. In transferring this authority to His followers, Jesus was fulfilling His promise when He said to Peter, "I will give you the keys to the kingdom" (Matt. 16:18–19)

Notice that Jesus said He has been given all authority, which means Satan has none. Many believers get all nervous about the devil doing this to us or that to us, but Jesus said all authority had been given to Him. That word *all* is a very interesting word in the original Greek. It means "all"! Satan does have some power but he has no authority. You might wonder why then does Satan still seem to wreak havoc in the world? There are still many evidences of the fall of mankind— things like sickness, disease, and death—in the world. How does this happen and where does he get his authority? The same way he got it in the garden. He talks to us until we come in agreement with him. When we believe his lies we give authority to the liar. It is time for us as believers to stop giving away the authority that Jesus delegated to us. He gave us back the keys of the kingdom and it's time for us to step into and walk in the kingdom authority He has delegated to us.

We have already noted that Jesus' primary assignment was to destroy the works of the devil. But for the first thirty years of Jesus life we have no record of Him doing anything to destroy the works of the devil. It wasn't until His baptism and filling with Holy Spirit that He became empowered to fulfill this assignment. Then He regularly destroyed the works of the devil by healing the sick, casting out demons, raising the dead, etc.

Jesus told His followers, "As my Father has sent Me, I also send you" (John 20:21, NAS). In other words, My assignment to destroy the works of the devil is now your assignment to destroy the works of the devil. How were they going to do this? In Acts 1:8 Jesus told the apostles that they would receive power when the Holy Spirit came upon them. They would be empowered for this assignment the same way Jesus was empowered for this assignment. In Acts 2, we see that power coming upon them at Pentecost when the Holy Spirit was poured out and they began to do what Jesus had done. They healed the sick, raised the dead, and demonstrated the truth that the kingdom was at hand. The assignment has not changed. We, too, are called to destroy the works of the devil. As believers today, we, too, can be filled with the same Holy Spirit and experience the same power and dominion over the enemy that Jesus demonstrated when He destroyed the works of the devil. Just as Jesus was physically incarnate in a human body when he walked on this earth, there is a sense in which He is still incarnate in a body today. The body of Christ exists today. It is just in a different form. Now He is here in the form of the church, and as His body we are both called and empowered to take authority over the enemy the same way He did when He was walking on the earth.

Most of the church has never experienced this in our day. The church today is operating in something less than this same power and authority. Most believers today are not anticipating Jesus moving through us in this kind of power, and most don't even know that they can have this kind of power. The church today is not operating in all of its kingdom privileges. But our assignment has not changed. We have been delegated authority by the King to live under the rule and reign of God today, in the kingdom today, and to demonstrate that authority by destroying the works of the devil just as Jesus did. We have been called to declare the words that the kingdom is at hand and also do the works that Jesus did that demonstrate the kingdom is at hand. The whole underlying concept of this kingdom teaching is that we have been called not only to teach the message about the kingdom but also to do the ministry that demonstrates the kingdom.

For over twenty years of ministry, I had never witnessed a demon manifest. In fact, I had been told these things no longer exist today. However, as I began to recognize the power and authority that we have been given over the enemy, I began to witness much in the way of demonic activity. I remember my first encounter clearly. One day I was called along with a couple of other pastors on my church staff to go pray at the home of a family in our church. Their teenage son was not sleeping well. He seemed tormented at times, and they asked if we could come pray over their house and their son and anoint the place with oil. As we began to go through the house and pray and ask God to reveal any open doors for the enemy to have a foothold in this home, we noticed that the young man became more and more agitated. His eyes were dark. His face seemed to be scrunched up in a scowl. And he kept making weird, guttural noises. By this time I had come to believe theologically that demonization still occurs today, but I had never experienced it firsthand. I was perceptive enough to know this young man's behavior was not normal. Something strange was going on with him. I looked the young man in the eye and asked him to say, "Jesus is Lord." At this he became even more agitated. His eyes rolled back in his head and he said in a deep gruff voice that was definitely not his own, "Nice try." He then became very physically aggressive. The two pastors that were with me were each about 300 pounds and this boy was probably 180 pounds dripping wet, but they couldn't hold him down. He kept flailing and fighting and seemed to have a supernatural strength.

As I said, I had been in ministry for over twenty years but I had never been trained in my conservative Bible college background or in my years of experience for an encounter like this. So, I did the only thing I knew to do. I went to the hallway outside the room where this was all going on and called a Pentecostal pastor friend. I was pretty sure she had dealt with this before. Over the phone, she gave us a crash course in taking authority over the demons. So we commanded the demons in Jesus' name to stop tormenting this young man and to leave him alone. Immediately the young man became calm.

Now I am not one to believe there is a demon behind every bush, but from that time on, I began to encounter demons regularly. Another of my early experiences with the demonic realm took place in a deliverance session with a man who came from an America Indian background. He had come to me in desperation because he couldn't sleep at night. He heard voices and felt constantly tormented and found himself doing things that seemed beyond his control. As we talked that day, we discovered that he had an uncle who was the medicine man of their tribe. The medicine man's role is basically to bring the spirit world to assist people in the tribe with things like healing. This was a connection to the demonic spirit world, and as a result this man became exposed to many evil spirits. In the course of that meeting, as we called out several demons, several spoke to us and identified themselves by name and the man at times began to sweat profusely and become violent and physically ill. We took authority over the demons one by one, bound them up, and cast them out of this man; and they stopped abusing him. After multiple demons left, the man's countenance changed drastically as he began to radiate with joy and peace. This is the kingdom!

Another young lady I encountered came into our church one year just before Christmas. She looked exhausted and disheveled. Her fiancé, who was with her, told us that she had been acting really weird and talking in this strange deep voice that was not hers. I tried to get her to read from the Bible and she couldn't. Her countenance would change and she became violent and a deep voice, definitely not the voice of this sweet young lady, came out of her swearing profusely. Again, I took authority over the demons in Jesus name and cast them out and she left a much happier, much freer young lady. I saw her in church in the coming weeks and she didn't even look like the same girl. She was beautiful, radiant, and free. This is the kingdom!

These were just a few of my beginning experiences with the demonic, and I have encountered this on a more regular basis ever since then. For over twenty years of ministry I had never witnessed this, but now I seem to see it regularly. Why? Because now I'm aware that there is a real clash of kingdoms going on and we have been given authority as believers over the kingdom of darkness. We shouldn't be surprised because Jesus told us, "I have given you authority to trample on snakes and scorpions and to overcome all the power of the enemy; nothing will harm you" (Luke 10:19). We are called to take authority over the kingdom of darkness because we live in the kingdom of light. He has delegated to us His authority over the enemy.

Chapter 5

HEALING POWER

JESUS ALSO DEMONSTRATED the kingdom was at hand through the healing of disease. It was important for Jesus to demonstrate the kingdom through healing. In order to understand why healing is a demonstration of the kingdom, we first must understand why disease is a part of this world. It is almost impossible for you and me to imagine a world that does not include sickness and disease. It's almost impossible for us to comprehend a world that doesn't include hospitals, pharmacies, doctors' offices, surgery centers, cancer treatment centers, radiation, and chemotherapy. And while it is almost impossible for us to fathom a world that does not include all these things, that is exactly the way God created the world in the beginning. When God created Adam and Eve and placed them in the Garden of Eden, as unbelievable as it may seem to us, the entirety of their lives and daily experiences were all disease-free. They experienced the world as God created it to be and desire of it to be—a place of physical perfection.

When Satan came and tempted Adam and Eve to rebel against God's kingdom, and they sinned, Satan usurped the authority that God had delegated to mankind to rule in this world; and all of a sudden this world became Satan's kingdom. And with his kingdom came sickness, disease, and pain—physically, emotionally, spiritually, you name it. And our world, ever since, has been plagued with physical dysfunction. So it only makes sense that when Jesus showed up on the scene, He would not only announce that He had come to restore the kingdom of God and bring an end to the kingdom of Satan, but that He would demonstrate the kingdom by restoring physical health to people wherever He went.

Over and over again in the Gospels, we read about how Jesus brought physical healing to those facing disease. Matthew 9 is one chapter that focuses on the healing ministry of Jesus. And Matthew ends this chapter with a little summary statement. This particular statement is mirrored several times in the Gospel accounts.

> Jesus went through all the towns and villages, teaching in their synagogues, proclaiming the good news of the kingdom and healing every disease and sickness.
> —MATTHEW 9:35

What message did He preach? The good news of the kingdom. What ministry did He do? He healed every disease and sickness. In doing so, He was demonstrating that He had come to usher in the kingdom.

I don't believe Matthew's intent was to say that Jesus healed every person. There were still sick people in the world while Jesus was here. I think what Matthew wants us to know is that there was no sickness or disease over which Jesus did not have authority. I don't believe when Jesus went into a town He automatically healed everybody who was sick. That may have happened at times, but not always. For instance, in John 5:1-15 tells of when Jesus went to the pool of Bethesda where he healed a lame man who had been lying at that pool for thirty-eight years. The people lay at this pool day after day because they believed that occasionally an angel would come and stir the water and the first person in the water would be healed. If this man had been sitting there for thirty-eight years waiting for healing and the people believed that healing happened when the waters were stirred, you can imagine that there would have been many people gathered at the pool that day waiting for their opportunity to be healed. In fact, John wrote that the blind, lame, and paralyzed were all brought to the pool. But out of all of the people there that day, Jesus asked just one man, "Do you want to get well?" (v. 6) and proceeded to heal him because He realized that was what the Father was doing. The Jewish leaders were upset with all this, so "Jesus gave them this answer: 'Very truly I tell you, the Son can do nothing by himself; he can do only what he sees his Father doing, because whatever the Father does the Son also does'" (v. 19).

Matthew details some very specific healings in this chapter. Jesus had just been teaching His disciples about fasting. They were having a conversation and got interrupted by a ruler of a local synagogue: "While he was saying this, a ruler came and knelt before him and said, 'My daughter has just died. But come and put your hand on her, and she will live'" (Matt. 9:18). Can you imagine a deeper pain for a father than to watch his daughter pass away? Jesus got up and went with him, and so did his disciples. Verse 20, says, "Just then a woman who had been subject to bleeding for twelve years came up behind him and touched the edge of his cloak." In Luke's gospel account, we learn that when she touched Jesus' cloak, she was instantly healed (8:30). There was a huge crowd following Jesus. Why was there a huge crowd? Because He was on His way to supposedly raise a little girl from the dead. You would go to that show, wouldn't you? You would even buy a ticket. You would be thinking, "If He's about to raise some-body from the dead, I want to witness that!" So they crowded around Jesus and followed Him, and this one woman touched Him. Jesus amazingly asked the question, "Who touched me?" (v. 45). The disciples just laughed at Him. "What do you mean who touched you?

Jesus, everybody is touching you! There are people crowded all around you." But He knew this touch was different. He had felt healing power go out from His body. He turned and looked at the woman and said, "Daughter, your faith has healed you" (v. 48). She was healed before Jesus could even heal her. And then we read in Matthew 9:27 that Jesus healed two blind men and gave them sight. Later in this chapter we read about a demonized man who was mute and could not talk. Jesus rebuked this dumb spirit and healed this man and instantly he began to talk (vv. 32–33).

Matthew intended to communicate in his summary statement that everywhere Jesus went, healing was a part of what he did. He would talk about the kingdom and then demonstrate the kingdom through healing. He healed many thousands of people—so many that they are not nearly all recorded in Scripture. Matthew, Mark, Luke, and John tell of about thirty-five specific people who were healed in addition to times where they say multitudes came and He healed all of the sick. If you were to lay those accounts side by side, read through them, and think about them, you would come to a few conclusions and observations about Jesus' healing ministry.

First, there was absolutely no formula to the way Jesus healed. I believe he did that on purpose. If he always did A, B, C, and D, and people were healed, we would copyright it, put it in a book, and use it as a formula to heal the sick everywhere we went. We would put God in a box and expect Him to act the way we expect Him to. But as we look at the way Jesus healed, we see there was no formula whatsoever. Sometimes Jesus spoke a word and sometimes He was silent. Sometimes He touched a person and sometimes He healed from long distance; He spoke it in one place and in another geographical region someone was healed. The power that flowed through Him was amazing. Sometimes He did it among a crowd so that people could watch and be amazed. Sometimes He did it in private, pulling someone to the side. Sometimes when Jesus healed, the people that needed healing asked, "Lord, would you heal me? Can You heal me? Are You able to heal me? I believe, but help my unbelief." And sometimes Jesus healed without us knowing if the person ever asked for it or even wanted it. There was no formula.

Once He made mud with His spit and rubbed it on a blind man's eyes (John 9:6). One time when Jesus went to heal a man who was blind, it took Him two tries to finish it. The first time the man opened his eyes and saw men who looked like trees. Then it says Jesus touched him again and he was able to see (Mark 8:22–25). How can it take the Son of God two tries? What we clearly see is that there was no formula in the healing ministry of Jesus whatsoever. Sometimes faith plays a significant part. He said to the woman who touched His garment, "Your faith has made you well" (Mark 5:34, NAS). But sometimes it appears as though faith is completely absent. We don't know, but sometimes it seems like Jesus healed only to give somebody faith. There was no formula to how Jesus healed, and I think that's important.

Sometimes physical sickness is intimately linked with a demonic presence. In Matthew 9 when Jesus healed this mute man, it says the reason he could not speak was that he was demonized. In Luke 4 we read of another such encounter.

> Jesus left the synagogue and went to the home of Simon. Now Simon's mother-in-law was suffering from a high fever, and they asked Jesus to help her. So he bent over her and rebuked the fever, and it left her. She got up at once and began to wait on them.
> —LUKE 4:38–39

Jesus had gone home with Simon Peter, and when they arrived at his home they found that his mother-in-law was sick. Peter must have looked at Jesus and said something to the effect of, "Jesus, I've seen you heal all these sick people. Will you heal my mother-in-law?" So Jesus ministered to her.

Peter's mother-in-law was sick with a fever; and Luke says something interesting, "He rebuked the fever." The word that is translated "rebuke" here can again literally be translated as "stop it!" When Jesus spoke to demons, He often rebuked them and said, "Stop it!" You may wonder, "What relationship is there between a demon and a fever? A fever doesn't have any personality. How do you speak to a fever?" Yet, Jesus did it. He rebuked the fever. You may think perhaps Jesus was just caught up in the viewpoints of His day, but I think Jesus knew everything. The Scriptures reveal the fullness of His knowledge. What I believe is that Jesus recognized there was a spirit behind this fever that was causing the fever to manifest. Look at the words that Luke used: "He bent over her and rebuked the fever." He spoke to the fever and said, "Stop it!" He saw something in that fever that was beyond the fever itself. There was a demonic presence that was causing it. Luke records that when he bent over her and rebuked the fever, it left her immediately. It doesn't say the fever died down or that the fever had cooled. It says the fever left. How does a fever get up and leave? In this case, the fever got up and left because it was caused by a demonic spirit.

Let's consider one more example found in Luke 13 that makes the link between demonic oppression and the disease clear: "On a Sabbath Jesus was teaching in one of the synagogues, and a woman was there who had been crippled by a spirit for eighteen years. She was bent over and could not straighten up at all" (Luke 13:10–11). Luke was an incredible historian who paid very careful attention to detail. But even more important to remember is that Luke was also a physician. He seemed to be especially drawn to those stories about Jesus healing someone. The physician recognized there was something different about what this woman was dealing with. He recognized that there was a demonic oppression that was causing this illness. I would imagine that Luke probably had some working knowledge of curvature of the spine. As a physician it was not foreign to him, yet he saw in this situation something beyond the actual physical infirmity; and he said that a spirit had caused this woman's condition.

> When Jesus saw her, he called her forward and said to her,
> "Woman, you are set free from your infirmity." Then he put his
> hands on her, and immediately she straightened up and praised

God. Indignant because Jesus had healed on the Sabbath, the synagogue leader said to the people, "There are six days for work. So come and be healed on those days, not on the Sabbath."

—LUKE 13:12–14

They had just seen a woman experience a miraculous healing, a woman who they no doubt knew very well. She undoubtedly had walked into that synagogue regularly unable to even stand up straight to raise her face to her God because the deformity in her spine caused her to be so hunched over. Jesus instantly straightened out her spine and all the religious leaders could say was to do it on another day. What happens when God operates outside of your box? The synagogue ruler didn't expect God to do heal on that day in that way and there was no place in his theology to put it. All he could do was respond with a religious idea by saying, "Don't do it on the Sabbath," instead of looking this woman in the eye and rejoicing that she had been set free.

Apparently Jesus felt the same way about their response, because the next verse says,

The Lord answered him, "You hypocrites! Doesn't each of you on the Sabbath untie his ox or donkey from the stall and lead it out to give it water? Then should not this woman, a daughter of Abraham, whom Satan has kept bound for eighteen long years, be set free on the Sabbath day from what bound her?" When he said this, all his opponents were humiliated, but the people were delighted with all the wonderful things he was doing.

—LUKE 13:15–17

We need to be careful here. We can't jump to a quick conclusion and say, "All curvatures of the spine are caused by demons." That would not be valid. However, we do have to recognize that this particular curvature of the spine was caused by a demon because the scripture identifies it as such. I think it is fair to say that at least some sickness has a direct correlation with some sort of demonic presence.

When we look at the different healings Jesus did, at least eight or nine times the Gospel writers include that there was a demonic spirit linked with the sickness. That was not the case every time, but it definitely happened on a regular basis. This really should not surprise us when we understand that sickness is part of Satan's kingdom. Sickness and disease were never God's intention for mankind in the first place, and Jesus demonstrated His authority over Satan's kingdom through healing. The healing ministry of Jesus was a physical demonstration that He came to usher in the kingdom.

Let's put it back in the context of the kingdom. Jesus came with a message that we can live in the kingdom of God now. We can leave the kingdom of darkness and enter the kingdom of light. We can stop living under the enemy's control and start living in a new kingdom— the kingdom of God. Part of Jesus' ministry involved casting out of demons; and furthermore, part of that ministry was the healing of disease. We see there is a very real conflict between two kingdoms taking place—the kingdom of God on the one hand and the kingdom of the god of this world on the other hand. When Jesus saves us, He saves all of us. He saves not just our spirits but our bodies as well.

This demonstration of the kingdom over disease is a problem for many of us because we have been raised with a Western mindset that is very scientific. It is hard for us to recognize or even believe in the supernatural. But this is the kingdom. Every time we come into contact with someone who is oppressed by the enemy through sickness, we are called to break the power of that spirit in the name of Jesus and command that spirit of sickness to leave. That is called kingdom warfare. That is called taking authority over the enemy. Paul says we are supposed to be aware of the schemes, the strategies of the enemy (2 Cor. 2:11); but lets face it, in our Western culture most of us don't understand the strategies of the enemy because most of us don't even recognize there is such a thing as a spirit world. Even the church today often ignores the spirit world. And religion has stripped the church of living in kingdom power and taught us to believe that we can't expect to take authority over disease the way Jesus did. We have in effect been taught the doctrines of demons. But, when we understand the kingdom, we must see our assignment has not changed. What is our assignment? To destroy the works of the devil. How do we destroy the works of the devil? Jesus put it this way, "Heal the sick, raise the dead, cleanse those who have leprosy, drive out demons. Freely you have received; freely give" (Matt. 10:8). That is our assignment. We have been called to advance the kingdom, not just by preaching the message of the kingdom but also by doing the ministry of the kingdom, and part of that ministry involves healing the sick.

I have begun to see many instances of disease bowing its knee to King Jesus. One day a man who could barely walk came into to our church and left running and dancing. What happened? Gout bowed its knee to King Jesus. Heaven had invaded earth.

A man came to our men's group and announced that for years he had been unable to hear out of one of his ears. We prayed and took authority over that deafness and thirty minutes later I received a text from him saying that he had just gotten off the phone with a friend holding the phone up to the ear that he previously could not hear out of. What happened? The kingdom of heaven invaded this earth.

A woman in our church with rheumatoid arthritis woke up every morning with incredible pain. After a word of knowledge and receiving prayer at a conference we attended, her pain was gone. What happened? Arthritis bowed its knee to King Jesus. Jesus said He came to destroy the works of the devil (1 John 3:8) and then He turned to us said, "As the Father sent me, I also send you" (John 20:21). So it's not really that complicated. That is our assignment.

Let me tell you about Katherine. From birth she suffered from numerous earaches and ear infections that many young children seem to battle with. But by the time she was four years old, her parents realized it was something more. She was sick all of the time and would take the antibiotics that were supposed to take care of the problem; but every time she completed a course of antibiotics, she would continue to be sick. The doctors ran a battery of tests checking for things like immune disorders, cystic fibrosis, and a long list of other things.

Every time the doctors thought they had diagnosed the problem, it would turn out to be a wrong diagnosis.

During her second sinus surgery, the doctors did a lung biopsy and tested for a very rare genetic disorder—not because they thought she had it, but just to rule it out. They soon received the test results; and to their surprise, the results were positive. Katherine had what is called primary ciliary dyskinesia or PCD.

PCD is a genetic disease that causes the cilia—the hair-like structures that exist in our lungs, brain, and sinuses, and function as a filtration system—to become stiff. A person with this disease becomes highly susceptible to any viruses or bacteria they come in contact with. Katherine was diagnosed with this disease, and her parents were told she would have it for the rest of her life. There is no cure for PCD, and the best they could hope for was to try to prevent infections through a constant regimen of steroids and antibiotics and to try to keep her environment as sterile as possible. They were told that eventually PCD would compromise her hearing and cause her lungs to harden and she would not have a normal life span. At some point in the future, she would need a partial lung removal and maybe even a lung transplant.

If she wanted to go to school and be around other children, she would need to do things like use a sinus rinse with a water pick three times a day. She so desperately wanted to attend school and play sports like all the other children that she willingly did whatever it took. Her parents decided there was nothing else to do but trust her to God's care and pray for a miracle. Through all the doctor visits, her mom took her Bible and read Scripture and prayed. Instead of feeling sorry for herself, Katherine would minister to other kids who were in worse shape. There was one little boy who was petrified and didn't want to have a needed surgery. Katherine ministered to him and told him, "It is okay. The last time I was in surgery, Jesus held my hand the whole way through."

Katherine continued to get worse. In about third grade she was having another surgery and had been on steroids so long that she found herself very swollen and sore to the touch. Many mornings she would wake up throwing up, and her parents would have to do cupping to clear her lungs just so she could go to school; but she was willing to do whatever it took to be like the other kids.

Her parents asked the doctors if there was anywhere they could move that would improve her condition, but they told her there really wasn't. Children with PCD live all over the world in many different environments. But as they prayed, God laid it on their hearts to move from Texas to Denver. They would need to find new doctors, but they soon discovered that one of the leading experts on PCD in the world was in Denver. The doctor visits continued and her mom continued to take her Bible and read and pray at each visit. That brought incredible peace in the midst of a very trying ordeal, and they continued to trust in God's plan, knowing that God loved Katherine more than they ever could.

After six weeks of being in Denver, the change in Katherine was amazing. She was no longer on antibiotics. When they returned to Texas, her grandmother cried and said, "I know you are never coming home because I have never seen my granddaughter look this well." In the next two years, Katherine was only on antibiotics four times. She began to run and play competitive soccer.

They returned to the doctor for another one of their regular checkups to see how the disease was progressing. As usual, while the doctors performed the tests, her mom prayed; and it was then that she heard God speak to her and say, "Because of faith you have this miracle." And her mom had an instant peace and confidence that the test results were going to be good.

They did the usual tests three times and then sent her for a CAT scan. They sent Katherine and her mom out for lunch while they looked at the results. When they returned, the nurse said, "We're going to let you go, but the doctor wants to talk with you first." When the doctor came in he said, "You do know that PCD is genetic, right? It's part of who she is. It's part of her makeup. It can't be changed. It can't be undiagnosed." All the time Katherine's mom was thinking to herself, "We are in year six of this. I probably know as much about PCD as you do. Why are you telling me this?"

The doctor continued, "There is really no explanation for these tests. A PCD patient's nitric oxide levels should be extremely low like hers have been in the past. But Katherine's is at the level of a highly trained athlete! Further, the spot on her lungs is gone. Her lungs are completely clear! There is no evidence of the PCD anywhere in her body. She is a perfect 10 year-old! I have no explanation for this."

Her mom said, "I have an explanation. God told me, 'Because of your faith you have this miracle.'" The doctor wasn't convinced and said, "We are going to send you home today, but we want to do a biopsy." A few months later the doctor called and apologized for taking so long; he proceeded to tell them that they had sent the biopsy to three independent labs and all three came back the same. She had normally working cilia, and she no longer had PCD. Only one explanation makes sense. PCD bowed its knee to King Jesus and heaven invaded earth and healed Katherine!

You may wonder, "What about those who don't get healed? Why do some get healed and others spend a lifetime battling debilitating sickness and disease?" I wish I knew the answer to that question. But here is what I do know. I know that God is good. And I refuse to sacrifice my belief in the goodness of God on the altar of personal experience.

Remember, the kingdom is both now and not yet. While we can live in the kingdom now, we will not see the kingdom in the fullest sense until Jesus returns and every sickness, pain, and disease is non-existent. In the meantime, I choose to keep praying and trusting and advancing the kingdom by destroying the works of the devil. That is our kingdom assignment.

Chapter 6

DEATH DEFEATED

ONE OF THE clear indications that Satan had usurped the authority that God delegated to mankind to rule and reign on the earth is the presence of physical death. God told Adam and Eve if they ate of the fruit of the forbidden tree they would surely die (Gen. 2:17). When they ate and sinned against God, both physical and spiritual death entered the world. If Jesus came to reintroduce the kingdom of God to earth, then one of the clear indications of that would be His demonstration of power and authority over death.

There are several stories recorded for us the Gospels where Jesus demonstrates authority over death. One of the most familiar is the story of Lazarus.

> Now a man named Lazarus was sick. He was from Bethany, the village of Mary and her sister Martha. Which Mary was this?

(This Mary, whose brother Lazarus now lay sick, was the same one who poured perfume on the Lord and wiped his feet with her hair.) So the sisters sent word to Jesus, "Lord, the one you love is sick."

—JOHN 11:1–3

Mary, Martha, and Lazarus were close friends of Jesus. They lived in Bethany, not far from Jerusalem; and it seems as though when Jesus would go to visit the city, He would stop by regularly to hang out with His close friends. They had the gift of hospitality, and Jesus loved to spend time in their home. There are some people who just have that special gift of making people feel welcomed in their home. From the very moment you walk through the door, they welcome you warmly and you feel as though they are genuinely glad you are there. They invite you help yourself the refrigerator, and there is always something good cooking on the stove. You feel at home in a place like that.

Then there are homes where you don't feel very welcome at all. You walk in and are immediately told to take off your shoes because the carpet is new, don't touch that, and don't eat that. You wouldn't feel very welcomed in a home like that. But Mary and Martha's home was an inviting home. We know Martha loved to cook, so whenever Jesus came by, she probably went in the kitchen and whipped up a feast for the Lord.

Mary would sit at the feet of Jesus and just hang on His words. Jesus loved these people and they were His close friends. (See Luke 10:38–41.) So when Lazarus became ill, Mary and Martha immediately sent a message to Jesus to let Him know that Lazarus was sick. They had seen Jesus perform miracles before, and they knew He had demonstrated authority over disease. They knew their brother was desperately ill, so they sent word to Jesus saying, "Your friend whom You love, our brother Lazarus, is very sick. In fact, if something doesn't happen soon, if You don't show up and do a miracle, he will be dead." That's what they wanted Jesus to do for them. They wanted Him to come heal their brother.

Notice the basis for their appeal. They didn't say, "Lord, because You have stayed at our house so often and have eaten so many meals at our table, You owe us this miracle. Come heal our brother." They didn't say, "Jesus, because we love You so much You should do this for us." They simply said, "Lazarus, whom You love, is sick." What a great reminder for us when we need a miracle. We should not demand that God do it for us because of what we have done for Him or say He should do it because we love Him. What we really need to remember is that God loves us more than we will ever love Him and He responds to us based on His love for us—not our love for Him.

> When he heard this, Jesus said, "This sickness will not end in death. No, it is for God's glory so that God's Son may be glorified through it." Now Jesus loved Martha and her sister and Lazarus. So when he heard that Lazarus was sick, he stayed where he was two more days.
>
> —JOHN 11:4–6

It's almost as though Jesus is saying, "Alright, I know things don't look good from your perspective and according to your timetable. You believe if I don't show up and do this miracle today, it's going to be too late; but I've got a different perspective. I've got a different time-table and I'm in no hurry. I'm going to take my time and wait a couple of days before I go because it really doesn't matter how quickly I get there. Whenever I show up it's never too late for something you think is impossible to be made possible. And when I'm through with this miracle, everyone will know that there is no way this could happen except for the hand of God at work. We've got to give God glory for that one."

> Then he said to his disciples, "Let us go back to Judea." "But Rabbi," they said, "a short while ago the Jews tried to stone you, and yet you are going back?" Jesus answered, "Are there not twelve hours of daylight? Anyone who walks in the daytime will not stumble, for they wee by this world's light. It is when a person

walks at night that they stumble, for they have no light." After he had said this, he went on to tell them, "Our friend Lazarus has fallen asleep; but I am going there to wake him up." His disciples replied, "Lord, if he sleeps, he will get better." Jesus had been speaking of his death, but his disciples thought he meant natural sleep. So then he told them plainly, "Lazarus is dead, and for your sake I am glad I was not there, so that you may believe. But let us go to him."

—JOHN 11:7–15

I'm sure the disciples were thinking at this point, "It's too late Jesus. Mary and Martha asked You to do a miracle and heal their brother, but You dillydallied around here for two days and didn't go and now it's too late. You just said Yourself, he is dead." Furthermore, the disciples really didn't want to go to Bethany. Bethany is just on the other side of the Mount of Olives right outside the city of Jerusalem. The last time Jesus had been there, He had gotten in a heated toe-to-toe conversation with the Pharisees, who had picked up stones planning to stone Jesus to death; but He had managed to slip away from them. Now Jesus is suggesting that they make a trip back to that area. The disciples decided they like living too much so that didn't seem to be a very good idea to them.

Thomas spoke up and said what the rest of the disciples were probably thinking, "Let us also go, that we may die with him" (v. 16). He's being kind of sarcastic and basically saying we are going to get killed if we go there.

On his arrival, Jesus found that Lazarus had already been in the tomb for four days. Bethany was less than two miles from Jerusalem, and many Jews had come to Martha and Mary to comfort them in the loss of their brother. When Martha heard that Jesus was coming, she went out to meet him, but Mary stayed at home. "Lord," Martha said to Jesus, "if you had been here, my brother would not have died."

—JOHN 11:17–21

Let me paraphrase this for you: "Where have You been Jesus? We trusted You to do a miracle and heal our brother. We have been bragging about Your wonder-working power to all our friends. This was the perfect opportunity for You to display Your power and show these people that the kingdom is at hand—to show them that You are the Son of God and have come to take authority over disease. And You come walking in four days later? You're too late." Martha was hurt and disappointed.

Many of us can relate to the disappointment that Martha felt and expressed. At times like this thoughts and questions run through our minds, such as, "God, I have been praying for this miracle. I have trusted You to do this miracle and yet nothing has happened. Are You there, God? Are You even real? And if You are real, and You're not doing what I'm asking You to do, are You good? And if You are there and You are good and You still aren't doing anything, then do You really have the power to do something about my situation? If You can, then why aren't You?" Those are real questions that run through our minds when we don't immediately get the miracle from God we are seeking. We say things like, "God, I just don't understand. Am I the problem? Is it You? What's wrong with this picture? Why haven't I gotten the miracle I wanted? Lord, where were You when my loved one died? Where were You when my marriage dissolved? Where were You when my parents divorced? Where we You when my job ended? Why didn't You intervene in this situation before it was too late?" Those are questions that have come to many of our minds when we don't understand.

Something worth noticing in this story is that Jesus didn't correct or rebuke Martha for what she said. He could have said, "Martha, why are you talking to Me like that? Don't be disrespecting Me, Martha." I think He didn't correct her because it was good that she was talking to Him. When something happens that doesn't make sense, don't run from God, run to God. You might think if you go to Him and tell Him what you really think He might not like what you have to say.

But notice that Martha was honest with Jesus about her feelings. I believe He wants us to be honest with Him well.

Lazarus had been dead for four days. Now there is dead and then there is really dead, and Lazarus was really dead. Some of the rabbis of Jesus' day taught that a person was not really dead until after three days. The general thinking was that for the first three days the soul would hover over the body intending to reenter it. After three days, death was considered irreversible.

One of my favorite television shows in recent years was "24." If you watched that show, you know that every time you think Jack Bauer is dead, he was never really dead. You always knew that somehow, someway he would get a shot, or something would happen that allowed him to get back up and start fighting the bad guys again. You thought he was dead, but he wasn't really dead.

Well four days dead is pretty dead, even according to the rabbis. Martha heard that Jesus had arrived, and she left the house to come out to meet Him. The disappointment in her voice is unmistakable, "Lord, if You had been here, my brother would not have died. Lord, I asked You to do a miracle. We called on You to do a miracle, but You took Your sweet time getting here and now it's too late for a miracle. My brother is dead." She was disappointed. But then notice the next verse. Even though she was disappointed, she hadn't lost faith in Jesus.

> "But I know that even now God will give you whatever you ask."
> Jesus said to her, "Your brother will rise again." Martha answered,
> "I know he will rise again in the resurrection at the last day."
> Jesus said to her, "I am the resurrection and the life. The one
> who believes in me will live, even though they die; and whoever
> lives by believing in me will never die. Do you believe this?" "Yes,
> Lord," she replied, "I believe that you are the Messiah, the Son of
> God, who is to come into the world."
>
> —JOHN 11:22–27

Mary and Martha needed a miracle. They asked Jesus to do a miracle and heal their brother, but it didn't happen. It would have been very easy for them to lose faith in Jesus, but that didn't happen; and in the end, they were going to witness a greater, more powerful miracle than they could have ever asked for or imagined.

> And after she had said this, she went back and called her sister Mary aside. "The Teacher is here," she said, "and is asking for you." When Mary heard this, she got up quickly and went to him. Now Jesus had not yet entered the village, but was still at the place where Martha had met him. When the Jews who had been with Mary in the house, comforting her, noticed how quickly she got up and went out, they followed her, supposing she was going to the tomb to mourn there. When Mary reached the place where Jesus was and saw him, she fell at his feet and said, "Lord, if you had been here, my brother would not have died."
>
> —JOHN 11:28–32

Notice Mary said the very same thing her sister said. "Lord, we asked You to do a miracle. We wanted You to heal our brother. We trusted Your power to do that miracle. We have seen You heal other people, but now it's too late. My brother is dead, and if You had just shown up sooner it would have been possible for my brother to be healed. But now it's impossible because he is dead." Her words were filled with incredible emotion, and we read, "When Jesus saw her weeping, and the Jews who had come along with her also weeping, he was deeply moved in spirit and troubled. 'Where have you laid him?' he asked. 'Come and see, Lord,' they replied. Jesus wept" (vv. 33–35). Think about that. Here is the Son of God who knows He is about ready to do the impossible. He's going to raise this dead man back to life again. He knew at any moment He could do it, and yet He wept. Why? Because that is how much He empathizes with people He loves. He was hurting for them. He was weeping because His people were hurting: "Then the Jews said, 'See how he loved him!' But some of them said, 'Could not he who opened the eyes of the blind man have kept this man from dying?'" (vv. 36–37).

Mary was weeping as she told Jesus about her brother. Jesus was so moved that He wept as well, and the people recognized that Jesus must have loved Lazarus. But that raised a question, "If He loved him so much, why didn't He show up in time to save his life? Why didn't He do a miracle for him?" And isn't that the question we often ask? We say, "God, if You love me so much, if You care about me so much, if You are such a good and loving God, then why aren't You giving me the miracle I need? Why is my marriage still in trouble? Why am I not getting the healing I need? Why is my financial picture so bleak? Why can't I find a job? If You can do all these miracles, can't You keep me from dying in this area of my life where I need a miracle?" But we are about to see that is never too late for the kingdom of God to invade the kingdom of darkness and bring victory.

> Jesus, once more deeply moved, came to the tomb. It was a cave with a stone laid across the entrance. "Take away the stone," he said. "But, Lord," said Martha, the sister of the dead man, "by this time there is a bad odor, for he has been there four days."
> —JOHN 11:38–39

Let's bring this to present-day reality. Your brother is sick and dying in the hospital. You ask Jesus to come and heal him but He doesn't show up. You have the funeral and He doesn't show up for the funeral either. Now it's four days later and your brother is already buried at the local cemetery and Jesus finally shows up and says, "Let's go dig him up." It would be shocking and morbid. I love the King James Version of this passage. It simply says, "He stinketh!" That says it all!

> Then Jesus said, "Did I not tell you that if you believed, you would see the glory of God?" [Something in Jesus words must have given Martha faith to act.] So they took away the stone. Then Jesus looked up and said, "Father, I thank you that you have heard me. I knew that you always hear me, but I said this for the benefit of the people standing here, that they may believe that you sent me." When he had said this, Jesus called in a loud voice,

"Lazarus, come out!" The dead man came out, his hands and feet wrapped with strips of linen, and a cloth around his face. Jesus said to them, "Take off the grave clothes and let him go."

—JOHN 11:40–44

Jesus actually proved He had power over life and death as He brought Lazarus back to life. What a demonstration that the kingdom of God was at hand! Satan's power and authority over death can't stop the invasion of the kingdom of God!

Jesus proved this ultimately through His own resurrection. The grave could not hold Him. Lazarus was resurrected only to die again some day. But Jesus was resurrected by the power of God proving once and for all that the kingdom of God had invaded the kingdom of Satan by taking authority over death. So every time Jesus took authority over demons, every time Jesus took authority over disease, every time He took authority over death, it was a demonstration that the kingdom of God was at hand.

There's an interesting passage recorded in Luke's gospel where John the Baptist sent his disciples to ask Jesus a question. John, as we have already seen, came preaching the message of the kingdom. He had already baptized Jesus and heard the voice of God declare, "This is my beloved Son, in whom I am well pleased" (Matt. 3:17, NKJV). He had identified Jesus as the Lamb of God who takes away the sins of the world. But now John found himself in prison, and it didn't seem like the kingdom was advancing the way that he understood the kingdom should advance. Here's the question, "Are you the one who was to come, or should we expect someone else?" (Luke 7:19) He was saying that he thought Jesus was the Messiah who came to usher in the kingdom, but now he wasn't so sure.

John's disciples went to Jesus to ask the question on John's behalf. Now when they arrived, they undoubtedly had to wait to even get to close to Jesus because crowds were following Him, pressing up against Him, wanting Jesus to heal their sick and deliver their demon-oppressed people. So by the time they actually got to Jesus, more than likely they had stood in amazement witnessing Jesus perform some incredible miracles. Finally, they got to Jesus and they asked John's question, "Are you the one who was to come, or should we expect someone else?" I love Jesus' response: "Go back and report to John what you have seen and heard: The blind receive sight, the lame walk, those who have leprosy are cleansed, the deaf hear, the dead are raised, and the good news is proclaimed to the poor" (v. 22).

When they returned to John, I'm sure they reported all these things that they had seen along with the message Jesus communicated. Jesus' response is very important because He clearly connected the miraculous things He did with a demonstration of the kingdom.

In the Old Testament the prophet Isaiah gave many prophecies concerning the Messiah, the King who was to come to usher in the kingdom. He gave us the portraits of the Messiah as a suffering servant (chapter 53), but Isaiah also gave general prophecies about the Messianic era and what would happen when the King arrived to usher in the kingdom. Those statements tie right in with Jesus' answer to John's disciples. Jesus told the disciples, "Go back and report to John that the blind receive sight and the deaf hear." Isaiah prophesied, "In that day the deaf will hear the words of the scroll, and out of gloom and darkness the eyes of the blind will see" (29:18).

Jesus said, "The lame walk." Isaiah prophesied the lame leap like a deer (35:6).

Jesus said, "The dead are being raised." Isaiah prophesied when the king, the Messiah arrived, "Your dead will live, LORD; their bodies will rise —let those who dwell in the dust wake up and shout for joy— your dew is like the dew of the morning; the earth will give birth to her dead" (26:19).

Jesus said, "The good news is being preached to the poor." Isaiah prophesied that when the Messiah came that these words would be true of Him: "The Spirit of the Sovereign LORD is on me, because the LORD has anointed me to proclaim good news to the poor" (61:1).

Jesus was clearly connecting the works that He did to the prophecies of Isaiah concerning the Messiah. He was communicating to John that He was the Messiah, the King, of whom Isaiah had spoken and He had come to usher in the kingdom of God to earth.

When it comes to raising the dead, you may wonder, "What does this have to do with the kingdom ministry we are to be involved in today?" Again, it is important to recognize that the kingdom is the rule of God on earth today. It is not only for today, but also for tomorrow. We live in the presence of the future. The kingdom is here now in its present form, but it is not in its complete form—yet. It will come in its fullness when Christ returns. But in Jesus' day as well as today, we can live in the kingdom now, today, although not in its complete form.

The ministry that demonstrates the kingdom must also accompany the message of the kingdom. Part of that ministry is not only the casting out of demons and healing the sick, but it is also the ministry of raising the dead. Again for most us who have been raised in a Western culture, we have a very scientific worldview of life. The idea of bringing the dead back to life again is so foreign to most of us because we see death as an irreversible process. Scientifically we would have great difficulty in demonstrating or arguing for anything different because we know that once you are dead you are dead. Yet here we see Jesus intervene and mess up all of our logical, scientific thinking by bringing someone back to life who was dead for four days! We have forgotten that Hebrews 2 tells us that Jesus came to "break the power of him who holds the power of death—that is the devil" (v. 14). The enemy held power over death; but when Jesus came to reintroduce the kingdom, He also destroyed the enemy's power over death.

Jesus wasn't the only one who raised people from the dead; but His raising of the dead established a pattern, a model if you will, that was then used by the apostles during their ministry to raise the dead. They learned to raise the dead by being with Jesus when He raised the dead.

You may wonder if we can still raise the dead today. My understanding is that both the model Jesus demonstrated for us and the mandate Jesus gave us to raise the dead has not changed. It is part of the kingdom! I believe there are times that any believer operating in kingdom power and authority may be called upon to exercise that power and authority over death. I have never personally raised the dead, but I refuse to allow my belief in what God wants to do or has the power to do through me at any given time to be limited by my personal experience. I believe it is clear in the context of kingdom warfare that there are times God may reverse what we consider irreversible and bring the dead back to life!

A friend of mine has personally experienced the raising of the dead. My friend Jim was in Africa preaching at a crusade. After the crusade they met at the home of one of the local pastors to try to figure out how to carry on the momentum from the crusade. As they were meeting, there was a knock on the door. Immediately the pastors were gripped with fear because this kind of meeting was illegal. When they opened the door, a man walked in carrying the dead body of his daughter in his arms. He carried with him a slip of paper with the pastor's address. He said, "The Holy Spirit gave me this address and said to bring my daughter here." He had carried her for four days from an outlying village through the hot African sun.

They told him to lay the girl's body on the huge coffee table in the middle of the living room. The pastors weren't really sure what to do, so they decided to pray in tongues. After about fifteen to twenty minutes of prayer, the girl's eyes fluttered and she sat up completely alive. All the skin on her body that had deteriorated during the trip in the hot son was instantly healed. The pastors were all amazed. The girl's dad sat in the corner of the room crying. The girl simply wanted to know, "Who are all these people, and why is my dad crying?"

One of the men left to drive the girl and her father back to their village. About thirty minutes later there was another knock on the door. They wondered if the pastor had experienced car trouble or something else was wrong. They answered the door and found two men carrying a homemade stretcher with the dead body of the son of one of the men. They proceeded to tell the pastors that the boy had been shot three days earlier. The Holy Spirit had spoken to his father and told him to get the body out of the morgue and go to this address. They prayed over the boy's body and after a time the body began to vibrate on the table. Eventually he woke up and came to life with the bullet hole still gaping open there in his chest. The amazing thing was the boy's father had so much faith that he had brought clothes for the boy to wear home. Now that's the kingdom!

Chapter 7

BORN AGAIN INTO THE KINGDOM

MARK FOUND HIMSELF in a cold dark basement. He had been alone in this basement for over thirty-five hours, high on crack cocaine. His life was spiraling out of control. He found himself crawling on the ground in search of another elusive rock of crack cocaine that he might possibly have dropped during the last thirty hours. He knew the drugs were gone, that the Joneses had arrived, and now it was just about time to experience hell.

In that moment, a thought came to him, "Maybe I need help. Man, do I need help. Wow, do I need help!" Filled with helplessness and frustration and not knowing where else to turn, he pounded his fist into the ground and said, "God, I need help!"

At that moment, Mark describes how two of the gentlest hands he had ever felt grabbed his shoulders and raised him up off the ground while he heard the voice of God quietly whisper, "My son, I have been waiting for you to ask for My help, but I had to have you ask before I could help you. It is time for you to call your brother and check into rehab. It's time to start your new life."

Mark spent 30 days in treatment becoming increasingly aware over time of the many battles he would have to face in order to recover. He had fought off past drug addiction successfully and stayed clean and sober from November 1989 until November 2005. He sought a higher power but did not know the God of the Bible. He found himself confused about life in general and spiritually completely dead.

In November 2005 Mark received a phone call from a friend inviting him to go to a Fellowship of Christian Athletes golf trip to Houston, Texas. Although skeptical, he accepted the invitation because the friend told him if he went he would send some remodeling business to his construction company.

Mark enjoyed playing golf and even getting to know some of the other guys. He wasn't quite sure what to think of this "cult of Christianity," as he liked to call it; and even though he returned home very confused, he knew something was stirring inside of him.

Four months later the friend who had invited him fulfilled his promise and was blessing Mark's construction company with numerous jobs. However, that was not the only remodeling business this friend had in mind. He was praying that God would remodel Mark's life.

Two weeks before Easter in March 2006, Mark sat with this friend at his house and asked him, "Are you a born again Christian?" When his friend said he was, Mark proceeded to ask him what kind of cult Christianity was. His friend sighed and assured him that this was not a cult at all and that he had been born again by trusting Jesus Christ as His Savior and Lord. He told him how he believed Jesus had died on the cross to pay the penalty for his sins and how three days later He rose from the dead and that through faith in Him we can be born again.

Mark looked at his friend dumbfounded and said, "That's it? That's all there is to it? Well, I believe that!" His friend responded, "Mark, that's the other part of this truth, you have to believe it with all your heart. When you do you are born again, a party begins in heaven in your honor as the words are believed in your heart and spoken from your mouth." That day Mark trusted Jesus with all his heart and surrendered his life to Christ. Mark and his friend embraced, excited about his new life in Christ and thinking about the party going on in heaven at that moment.

A few days later, Mark's phone rang at 6:30 a.m. He immediately became upset and agitated because he could not believe someone was actually calling him so early. Angrily, he grabbed his phone to see who was calling and it was a text message from his friend. It simply said, "The party is still going on!" Tears began to stream from Mark's eyes. Mark realized in that moment that he had indeed been born again. He was filled with so much joy and excitement inside and goose bumps and chills covered his body. From that time on, Mark's life has been completely different. God's grace has flooded him and drugs are no longer a part of his life. He is no longer the desperate man sitting in the dark alone in his basement looking for the next high. Everything in his life changed.

What happened in Mark's life to change Him? He didn't turn over new leaf. He didn't "get religion." He didn't just start going to church. He changed kingdoms. He moved from the kingdom of darkness to the kingdom of light. How does that happen? How can we move into God's kingdom today experiencing His rule and reign in our lives and exercising the power and authority that He has given to us?

Fortunately, Jesus tells us in John 3. In this chapter we read about guy Nicodemus who came to Jesus with some questions. Who was this guy Nicodemus? He was not an unbeliever. He was a Pharisee. We often think of Pharisees as self-righteous religious bigots who looked down their long religious noses at everyone else, and part of that is indeed true. But don't overlook the fact that in the Jewish community the Pharisees were considered the most moral, upright, God-fearing, and well-respected men in the community. When a man became a Pharisee, he took a vow to uphold every detail of God's law. So, as a Pharisee, Nicodemus was a very religious man. But Nicodemus was not only a Pharisee. He was also a member of the Jewish ruling council called the Sanhedrin. The Sanhedrin was kind of like the Jewish Supreme Court made up of seventy of the most brilliant legal minds in all of Israel.

Nicodemus approached Jesus in the middle of the night. Why? "He came to Jesus at night and said, 'Rabbi, we know you are a teacher who has come from God. For no one could perform the signs you are doing if God were not with him'" (John 3:2). One of the responsibilities this high court had was to deal with false prophets. There was concern among many of the religious leaders that Jesus might indeed be a false prophet, but Nicodemus was convinced otherwise. There was something different about Jesus from other prophets he had seen. He had witnessed Jesus doing incredible miracles, and he knew that there was an anointing of God on this man's life. Nicodemus wanted to know more about that. Although he understood that he knew a lot about God and had studied His law in detail, he obviously recognized that he didn't know God like this man Jesus knew God. He said, "God has to be with you because of the miraculous signs you perform."

"Jesus replied, 'Very truly I tell you, no one can see the kingdom of God unless they are born again'" (v. 3). Notice, Jesus responds by talking about the kingdom. Nicodemus hadn't asked about the kingdom. All he had done up to that point was address the fact that Jesus was performing miraculous signs, but Jesus addressed the kingdom. Why did He do that? Jesus referred to the kingdom because the miracles that Nicodemus was referring to were demonstrations of the kingdom. So when Nicodemus pointed out that the miracles indicated Jesus was a man from God, Jesus talked about the kingdom because those miracles demonstrated the kingdom.

Jesus went on to tell Nicodemus, "You won't understand this or ever make sense out of this unless you are born again." To which Nicodemus responded: "'How can someone be born when they are old?' Nicodemus asked. 'Surely they cannot enter a second time into their mother's womb to be born!'" (v. 4). Born again? That's ridiculous! A person can't be born a second time. You can't get back into your mother's womb and be born again.

Some of us have had premature children. Wouldn't it have been great to be able to put them back in the oven for a while until they were physically ready to face the world? Our son Joshua was born a little early, and he got some fluid in his lungs during delivery. He ended up spending several days in the hospital under a tent with oxygen. At that point we could have said, "Why don't you just put him back inside his mom for a few more days until he's ready to come out?" But we knew it didn't work that way. No one can get back into their mother's womb and be born again.

But Nicodemus was not a small child who had been born prematurely. He was a full-grown man, and Jesus said to him that he couldn't see the kingdom unless he was born again. Obviously Nicodemus was confused and wondered how that could possibly happen. Jesus answered, "Very truly I tell you, no one can enter the kingdom of God unless they are born of water and the Spirit. Flesh gives birth to flesh, but the Spirit gives birth to spirit. You should not be surprised at my saying, 'You must be born again'" (vv. 5–7).

Jesus cleared up Nicodemus' confusion. He was not talking about physical birth but about spiritual birth. You must be born of the water (physical birth) and you must be born of the Spirit (spiritual birth). To enter the kingdom, you must not only be born physically but you must be born again or be born spiritually.

John made sure we knew whom this guy Nicodemus was. He wanted us to recognize that this was no ordinary man. He was not a common criminal. This man Nicodemus was a Pharisee, a religious leader, and not just any Pharisee. He was a member of the Jewish ruling council. Yet to this religious and upright man, Jesus says, "You can't enter the kingdom of God unless you are born again." Don't miss this, because the same thing is true for every one of us. We cannot enter the kingdom of God through religion. We can't enter the kingdom of God through keeping God's law. We can't enter the kingdom of God through being a church leader. We can't enter the kingdom of God through being a good, moral person. What Jesus was saying to Nicodemus, and ultimately to each of us, is that we don't need religion, we need a new life. Spiritually Nicodemus was dead and could have no part in the kingdom of God unless he was born again. That is not only true of Nicodemus but of every single one of us. To enter the kingdom of God, we must be born again.

So what was Jesus talking about when He said we must be born again, and what does that have to do with the kingdom? To really understand this we again need to once again go back to the beginning, back to the Book of Genesis and the creation story. Remember that creation starts with God. God is by very definition the eternal and self-existent One. He alone has no beginning or no end. So, for all time God has existed and He alone has always been the Ruler of the kingdom of heaven.

God already reigned as King over this spectacular realm filled with angels who were there to serve Him and worship Him as King. At some point God decided to extend this heavenly kingdom into a new physical realm, so He created the earth. The kingdom of God and the kingdom of earth were one, and God was the King over both heaven and earth.

> Then God said, "Let us make mankind in our image, in our likeness, so that they may rule over the fish in the sea and the birds in the sky, over the livestock and all the wild animals, and over all the creatures that move along the ground." So God created mankind in his own image, in the image of God he created him; male and female he created them.
>
> —Genesis 1:26–27

There are two different words that are used in this verse to talk about God creating man. The first word is translated "make"; "Let us *make* man in our image." The second word is translated "created." We would probably look at those two words and think that the author is just saying the same thing two different ways, but when you look at the original language you find that is not the case. The words translated "make" and "create" are two different words in the original Hebrew with two distinct meanings.

The word translated "make" is the Hebrew word *asa*. This word means "to form from something that is already created." There is a part of man that is made from something that already existed. The word translated "created" is the Hebrew word *bara*, which means "formed from nothing." Man is both created and made. We are a composite of two distinct parts: something that did not already exist and something that already existed. So there is this sense in which we are created from nothing but also from something that already existed. This is very important for us to understand. Our spirit is the part of man that came from something that already existed. How do we know that? Because the spirit of man is created in the image of God. When God created mankind, He reached down inside of Himself and He pulled something out of Himself—out of His very own image— and He breathed into man His very own breath and man became a living being. God placed a spirit, made in His image, inside of mankind. It was this spirit given to mankind that allowed him to connect with God in a way that nothing else God created could connect with Him. Only man was made in God's image, given something of God himself, so he would be able to relate to and connect with God.[1]

Then to this man made in His image, God delegated the authority to take dominion and rule in His kingdom over the birds of the air, the fish of the sea, over all the animals, and ultimately over the earth itself. That word *dominion*, as we have already seen, speaks of the rule of the king over a territory. So what was God doing when He gave man dominion over the earth? He was giving mankind the legal authority to rule and reign on His behalf in this new territory called earth that He had created. This was a divine transfer of power where God declared, "I am going to put you in the position to rule and reign on My behalf in this new kingdom, this visible kingdom called earth that I have created." That was the purpose for which God created man.

So many of us struggle with our purpose in life, and yet God told us in the garden our purpose in life. We have been made in His image, with this spirit that is from God Himself; and He delegated to us the authority to rule and reign in this earthly kingdom on His behalf.

But you may wonder, "If we are created to rule and to reign on God's behalf on this earth, if we have been given dominion over creation, over the earth, why do I feel so powerless? Why am I not feeling like I'm living in this kind of power and authority?"

To answer these questions we have to ask another question. What else happened in the garden? Mankind committed the greatest act of treason that has ever been committed. God told Adam and Eve they were free to eat of any of the trees in the garden except for one, the tree of the knowledge of good and evil, and He told them the day that they ate of that tree, they would surely die (Gen. 2:16–17). Enter Satan, the fallen angel who had been kicked out of the kingdom of heaven and now ruled over a different kingdom, the kingdom of darkness. He tempted Eve with the opportunity to be like God. He came to Eve and said, "Did God say you couldn't eat the fruit of any of the trees in the garden?" She said, "No, just one. God said if we eat of the tree of the knowledge of good and evil we would surely die." Satan responded by casting doubt on God's character, "Did God really say that? That won't happen. What will happen if you eat the fruit of that tree is that you will be like God." (See Genesis 3:1–4.) In other words, you can have your own kingdom. You no longer will have to rule and reign under His delegated authority in His kingdom; but if you will eat the fruit of this tree, you can have your own kingdom. So Eve ate the fruit and she gave it to Adam who also ate the fruit. They sinned against God; and that sin was not merely disobedience, it was an act of treason.

What was the result of this sin? Satan usurped the dominion God had given to mankind. He became the prince of this dark world. God cursed the earth and said man was going to have to work by the sweat of his brow to get the soil to produce crops because now he would be fighting against thorns and thistles and women would have pain in childbirth. (See Genesis 3:16–19.) And the ultimate result of that sin was exactly what God said would happen. God said, "If you eat this fruit you will die." One thing we know is that physical death did come into the world at this point. The bodies of Adam and Eve started the process of dying, yet Adam lived over 900 years on the earth after he ate the fruit (Gen. 5:5).

So is there something else that God meant besides merely physical death that happened instantly in that moment? When God said, "If you eat of this fruit you will die," He was talking not just about that fact that physical death would now enter the world, He was talking about an immediate death of man's spirit. The spirit was that part of man made in God's image, that part of man that came from God Himself and allowed man to connect in relationship with God. Spiritual death entered the world at that instant. Mankind could no longer connect with God the way he had been created to connect with and relate to God. Adam and Eve were removed from the garden (3:23) and no longer could they fellowship with God the way they had previously because their spirit was dead.

And that is not just true of Adam and Eve, but the Bible tells us we have all sinned and fallen short of the glory of God and that the wages of sin is death (Rom. 3:23; 6:23). Our default mode is that because of sin, our spirit is dead. We cannot connect with God the way we were originally created to connect with God. So the only way that we can possibly connect with God is to be born again.

How is that possible? How can a person be born again? That's where Jesus comes into the picture. Jesus came as the second Adam, the Bible tells us (1 Cor. 15:45), to take back what Adam had lost. He came and lived a perfect, sinless life, thus qualifying Him as the sinless sacrifice who could pay our penalty of death by dying on the cross and conquering the enemy of death through His resurrection. In that He gave to each one of us the opportunity to receive His death, burial, and resurrection as a gift to pay for our sins; so that when His death is applied to our life, our spirit is born again and we can reenter that relationship with God. We can return to living in His kingdom, and we can fulfill that original assignment to take dominion, to rule and reign on God's behalf over the earth and over the kingdom of darkness. Through being born again, we are restored to the position that God created us to experience in the first place.

So when Jesus said to Nicodemus, "Unless you are born again, you can't enter the kingdom of God," what was He talking about? He was talking about his spirit needing to be reborn. He was saying to Nicodemus, and ultimately to each one of us as well, because of sin, your spirit is dead and you can't enter the kingdom of God unless your dead, lifeless spirit is infused by the very Spirit of God invading your life and connecting with your spirit and bringing it back to life again. Apart from that you can't really know God, you cannot relate to God, and you cannot be a part of His kingdom. So Jesus is saying that the only way that Nicodemus, or any human being, can enter the kingdom of God is to be born again.

Paul tells us the same thing:

> As for you, you were dead in your transgressions and sins, in which you used to live when you followed the way of this world and of the ruler of the kingdom of the air, the spirit who is now at work in those who are disobedient. All of us also lived among them at one time, gratifying the cravings of our flesh and following its desires and thoughts. Like the rest, we were by nature deserving of wrath.
>
> —EPHESIANS 2:1–3

Do you see why religion won't work? Do you see why we can't simply turn over a new leaf? Do you see why we can't enter the kingdom of God by keeping laws? Because we are dead. Our spirit is dead. That part of us that was created to relate to God is dead in transgression and sin.

Not only is our default mode that we are spiritually dead, also because of this we find ourselves in a kingdom already—the kingdom

Paul calls the kingdom of air, and it is under the rule or dominion of Satan. Our default mode is that we live in his kingdom. So without being born again, we are dead and we are part of Satan's kingdom.

Paul said that this applies to all of us. Just in case we wonder whether this really applies to us—this default mode of being dead in transgression and sin, he clearly tells us this is true of every one of us. We were all at one time spiritually dead, and we were all at one time part of Satan's kingdom.

He goes on,

> But because of his great love for us, God, who is rich in mercy, made us alive with Christ even when we were dead in transgressions—it is by grace you have been saved. And God raised us up with Christ and seated us with him in the heavenly realms in Christ Jesus, in order that in the coming ages he might show the incomparable riches of his grace, expressed in his kindness to us in Christ Jesus. For it is by grace you have been saved, through faith—and this not from yourselves, it is the gift of God—not by works, so that no one can boast.
>
> —Ephesians 2:4–9

This new birth originates with God. He is the only one who can resurrect your dead spirit to life by His grace. He sent Jesus to die in our place and pay the penalty for our sin, which is death, so we can be born again. This happens by faith. The Spirit of God draws our spirit to a point of faith. When we get to that point of faith and there is a personal transaction between us and God where we place our faith in Jesus and surrender our entire life to Him, at that moment God infuses us with his Holy Spirit and we are born again. That part of us that was dead because of sin then comes alive in Christ and we enter the kingdom of God—not someday in the future, but that very day. We are rescued from the kingdom of death and brought into the kingdom of life. We are transferred instantly from the kingdom of darkness and brought into the kingdom of light. All of a sudden there is a new relationship with a new King and everything about our life changes because we can now connect with and relate to God the way we were created to in the first place.

But it takes the work of the Holy Spirit for this to happen: "But the natural man does not receive the things of the Spirit of God, for they are foolishness to him; nor can he know them, because they are spiritually discerned" (1 Cor. 2:14, NKJV). In our natural state we can't understand the things of God. They seem like foolishness to us. This is because we are living in the kingdom of darkness and our spirit is dead. "The god of this age has blinded the minds of unbelievers, so that they cannot see the light of the gospel that displays the glory of Christ, who is the image of God" (2 Cor. 4:4). Naturally, we are blind to the things of God. They don't make sense. They seem like foolishness to us. Hearing the concept that we are sinners and need Jesus as our Savior will seem ridiculous to us without a work of the Holy Spirit. We will think, "I'm a good person, why would I need a Savior?" The idea that we will live eternally somewhere makes absolutely no sense to us at all. The man who is still dead in sin—who has not been infused by the Spirit of God and his spirit brought back to life so he can connect with and relate to God—this person cannot even understand the things of God. They won't make sense to him because the god of this age, who still rules the kingdom that he is living under, Satan, has blinded this person's eyes. Without a work of the Holy Spirit infusing our dead spirit and bringing about a new birth, we can't know God and the whole God thing will seem like foolishness.

Just a side note, this is why it is absolutely foolish for any Christ follower to witness to someone and tell them about the things of Christ without inviting the Holy Spirit to first of all work on their hearts. You aren't going to simply debate someone into the kingdom of God. You cannot lecture someone into the kingdom of God. You cannot argue someone into the kingdom of God. The only way any person's blind eyes can be opened and they can begin to see the things of God is by a work of the Holy Spirit on their hearts. He has to open their spiritual eyes to the things of God. So, it's much more important to pray than to lecture, to invite the Spirit to open the door of someone's heart than to try to beat the door down. It doesn't work. Jesus said, "Unless a man is born again, he cannot enter the kingdom of God" (John 3:5).

Now there are some other verses that we can't ignore that also speak of entering the kingdom of heaven. In Matthew 18 Jesus said, "Truly I say to you, unless you are converted and become like children, you will not enter the kingdom of heaven. Whoever then humbles himself as this child, he is the greatest in the kingdom of heaven" (vv. 3–4, NAS).

And in the Sermon on the Mount, Jesus said, "Blessed are the poor in spirit, for theirs is the kingdom of heaven" (5:3).

These verses both speak of humility as a means to enter the kingdom. This is not something different or additional from being born again. It is the means by which we receive the new birth. When the Holy Spirit works on our Spirit and opens our spiritually blind eyes so we can see the truth of our need for a Savior, then we have to decide, is this the truth? Am I really poor in spirit, spiritually bankrupt? Do I really need a Savior? Do I really want to become like a little child humbly and completely dependent on my Father, or do I want to continue living life the way I want to live it? It takes humility to receive the new birth.

This kind of humility was lacking in many of the religious leaders of Jesus' day. They thought they were in God's kingdom because they worked to the best of their ability to follow God's laws and keep His commandments. That is very much where Nicodemus found himself; but Jesus told him without the new birth, he was still spiritually dead. It was this kind of spiritual pride that was evidenced in the lives of the religious leaders that caused Jesus to say on one occasion, "I tell you the truth, the tax collectors and the prostitutes are entering the kingdom of God ahead of you" (21:31).

The only way we can enter the kingdom is by being born again. When the Spirit works on our hearts and causes us to recognize how dead we are and that we need new life—that we need to be born again, only those who are humble enough to recognize their own sinfulness and need for a Savior will enter the kingdom of God.

Chapter 8

POWER SOURCE OF THE KINGDOM

THE GOSPELS CLEARLY indicate that every time Jesus took authority over demons, every time Jesus healed diseases, every time Jesus raised someone from the dead and ultimately through His own resurrection from the dead, He was demonstrating that the kingdom of God was at hand. The primary message He preached demonstrated that the kingdom of God was at hand, and the ministry He did demonstrated that the kingdom was at hand. Again, we cannot separate the words that Jesus spoke about the kingdom from the works that Jesus did that demonstrated the kingdom. The two go hand in hand.

The question we need to ask next is, so what? What does that mean for you and me? You may be thinking: "Of course Jesus demonstrated authority over the demons, disease, and death, but He was the Son of

God. He may have come to preach the message of the kingdom and do the ministry of the kingdom but what about you and me? Do we have the same authority and power to advance the kingdom?"

Before we answer that, let's start with another question. Where did Jesus get the power to fulfill His assignment and destroy the works of the devil? By what power source did He drive out demons, heal the sick, and raise the dead? You might quickly answer, "He could do all those things because He was God in the flesh." Because He was God incarnate, we should expect there to be omnipotence displayed in His ministry. It is, of course, absolutely true that Jesus is, has been, and will always be God. There is no denying that in Him dwelt all the fullness of God (Col. 1:19; 2:9), meaning He had the ability to be omnipotent, omniscient, and omnipresent because of His divine nature. So, you might automatically assume that the power to destroy the works of the devil was just a by-product of Jesus being God in the flesh. But I do not believe that is how the Bible answers that question.

The apostle Paul wrote this as he tried to help us grasp the mystery of what we call the incarnation: "Who, being in very nature God, did not consider equality with God something to be used to his own advantage; rather, made himself nothing by taking the very nature of a servant, being made in human likeness" (Phil. 2:6–7).

Clearly these words affirm the deity of Christ. Paul wrote that Jesus was in very nature God. For all eternity Jesus has been and will be by very nature God. But also notice that even though Jesus always was and is God, in some way when He became a man He set that godly nature aside. He chose to willingly restrict Himself in the use of His divine attributes when he took on human form. As He emptied Himself of that divine nature, Jesus fully embraced the nature of a human being. Jesus became hungry (Matt. 4:2), thirsty (John 19:28), and tired (John 4:6). He limited himself while in a human body to only being at one place at one time. In His humanity, Jesus like other children "grew in wisdom" (Luke 2:52). In His adult ministry, He learned things through natural means (Heb. 5:8). He said of His second coming that He didn't know the day or hour but only His Father did (Matt. 24:36). Instead of depending on His own power for healing, He waited until the "power of the Lord was present" to heal the sick (Luke 5:17, NKJV). And there were times when, because of the unbelief of people, He was limited in His healing ministry (Mark 6:1–6; Matt. 13:58).

If Jesus had been only God and not fully man, then He would not have been qualified to die for the sins of mankind. He could not have really faced temptation and overcome if He was only God. It would have been no temptation. So, even though Jesus was fully God, He allowed Himself to take on the limitations of humanity in such a way that He did not heal the sick, prophesy, or minister out of His divine power; but He did minister in power. The sick were healed, the blind received sight, the lame walked, the deaf heard, demons fled, and death was conquered.

Where did this power come from? His power came from being filled with and complete dependence on the Holy Spirit. If Jesus did these things as God, we would be impressed. But if He did these things as a man, without sin, in right relationship with God, and empowered by the Holy Spirit, then He becomes an example for anyone without sin, in a right relationship with God, and filled with the Holy Spirit to follow.

In the Old Testament, Isaiah repeatedly prophesied that when the Messiah came He would be completely dependent upon the Holy Spirit.

> A shoot will come up from the stump of Jesse; from his roots a Branch will bear fruit. The Spirit of the LORD will rest on him— the Spirit of wisdom and of understanding, the Spirit of counsel and of might, the Spirit of knowledge and of the fear of the LORD—and he will delight in the fear of the LORD.
>
> —ISAIAH 11:1–5

Again we read, "Here is my servant, whom I uphold, my chosen one in whom I delight; I will put my Spirit on him, and he will bring justice to the nations" (Isa. 42:1).

> The Spirit of the Sovereign LORD is on me, because the LORD has anointed me to proclaim good news to the poor. He has sent me to bind up the brokenhearted, to proclaim freedom for the captives and release from darkness for the prisoners, to proclaim the year of the LORD's favor.
>
> —ISAIAH 61:1–2

Time and again Isaiah prophesied that the Spirit of the Lord would be upon the Messiah and that would be the source of His power to heal the sick, free the captives from demonic possession, and do all the other miraculous things that He did.

We have already noted that when Jesus came, He came with an assignment: "For this purpose the Son of God was manifested, that He might destroy the works of the devil" (1 John 3:8, NKJV). Yet, for thirty years there is absolutely no record of Jesus confronting the enemy or destroying His works. There were no healings, no miracles, no freeing people from demons, no raising anyone from the dead during this first thirty years. However, at His water baptism when the Holy Spirit came upon Him and baptized Him, everything changed. From that day forward He ministered in power with both the message and ministry of the kingdom. He showed us what a man without sin and completely dependent on the Holy Spirit could do. Is it then possible when a person puts their faith in Jesus as Savior, is filled with the Holy Spirit, and learns to become completely dependent on Him that they can also do what Jesus did? I believe so. But we must be filled with and plugged into the power of the Holy Spirit.

Imagine for a moment that you need a new refrigerator. You go to the local appliance store; and after examining all of the available models, you point to one and say, "That's it. That's the one I want." It is, of course, the top-of-the-line model and thus the most expensive unit on the floor. It has all the bells and whistles. This refrigerator promises to do things in your kitchen that no other refrigerator can do. It even has shelves that slide out automatically when you open the door so you can get what you need off the shelf without having to reach inside the refrigerator, and you are convinced beyond a shadow of a doubt this is the most awesome refrigerator known to mankind! And you think to yourself, 'I know it's expensive but I don't really care how much it costs. I want this amazing refrigerator in my kitchen filled with my food!" So you pay for the refrigerator and arrange for delivery later that same day. You can't wait. You are so excited for the arrival of your new awesome refrigerator. But then, on the way home it hits you. What good is a new refrigerator without lots of good food to fill it? You stop at the grocery store and buy all sorts of food so that when the refrigerator arrives you can make sure it is fully stocked. Everything goes as planned. They deliver it on time, you fill it with food and you're all set. That night you go to bed proud of your new purchase.

The next morning you wake up and go the pantry and get your cereal. You fill your bowl and make your way to your new state-of-the-art refrigerator. Before you even open the door, you notice the ice cream you put in the freezer has melted and started to run down and leak out the bottom of the door; and you wonder, "What's up with that?" You open the door to the refrigerator and pull out your milk and realize it's warm. You know this can't be good, but to make sure you remove the top off of the milk and take a good whiff. You feel your gag reflexes kicking in as you smell the sour milk. As you investigate further inside the refrigerator you find the vegetables are turning color and all of a sudden it hits you—this amazing, state-of-the-art, top-of-the-line, most expensive model on the floor refrigerator is not working. And you think, "I can't believe this! That store took my hard earned money and stuck me with a lemon; and now not only do I have a refrigerator that doesn't work, I have a refrigerator full of spoiled food and sour milk."

Immediately you decide that you need to call the appliance store, ask for the manager, and give him a piece of your mind—in Christian love of course. You get the manager on the line and you start to rant, "I gave you $10,000 good dollars for a brand-new, top-of-the-line, state-of-the-art refrigerator with all the bells and whistles; and you sold me a lemon! The refrigerator is not working and all my food is now spoiled!"

The manager asks you to calm down and assures you they want to make it right. "But," he says, "before we do anything, would you mind if I just ask you a few questions?" You agree.

First he asks, "Would you open the door and let me know if when you open the door the light comes on or not?" So you open the door and see nothing but darkness and inform him, "No, there is no light."

Next he asks, "Would you put your ear down by the bottom and see if you can hear a hum?" You get down on the floor and listen closely and inform the manager, "No, there is no hum. It is completely silent."

He then asks, "Can you kindly look in the back of the refrigerator and tell me if the cord is plugged in?" You take a look; and, lo and behold, the refrigerator is not plugged in! You get back on the phone and tell the manager, "I checked the cord and it's not plugged in, but for $10,000 that shouldn't matter!"

Then the manager says, "Let me explain something to you. Appliances are dependent in nature. While this refrigerator has all the component parts to deliver all the bells and whistles the manufacturer promised, it is not made to do it on its own. It needs to be empowered."

As we consider what it means to advance the kingdom, live in victory, and destroy the works of the devil by taking authority over things like sickness, pain, and death, we need to know that our manufacturer has promised all these bells and whistles. But the reality is we are dependent in nature. We need to be empowered. We must be baptized, filled with, washed, and overflowing with this permanent stream of living water flowing out of us called the Holy Spirit.

I have been in the church all of my life. I became a Christian as a child, studied in Bible college, and even served as a pastor for over twenty years before I understood or experienced the baptism of the Holy Spirit. I was taught that when a person receives Jesus as Savior they receive all the Holy Spirit there is and that there is no such thing as a baptism, greater filling, or release that can take place subsequently in the life of a believer that is different or distinct from that initial experience. However, as I dove back into studying Scripture on my own, I came to believe that what I had been taught is not what the

Bible taught but rather there is a clear promise of the baptism in the Holy Spirit that is distinct and different from conversion.

Beyond that scriptural study, I personally received the baptism of the Holy Spirit and began to speak in tongues and experienced a new power and anointing in my ministry beyond anything I had ever experienced before.

I truly believe the baptism of the Holy Spirit is what is missing in most evangelical churches in America today. That is why so many people are walking around living powerless Christian lives, talking about the words of the kingdom but not operating in the fullness of the kingdom. If we are going to live and operate in the fullness of both the kingdom message and kingdom ministry, we must be empowered by the Holy Spirit. I do not believe the baptism in the Holy Spirit is something the Bible is at all ambiguous about.

The first baptism we read of in the New Testament was not Spirit baptism but water baptism. There was a guy named John who did so much water baptism that they nicknamed him John the Baptist. That had nothing to do with his denomination. He didn't found the Baptist church. Literally, he was John the Baptizer. John was baptizing people in the middle of the Jordan River. He preached a simple message over and over again. You could fit it on a 3x5 card. "Repent, repent, repent. The kingdom is at hand, repent." And people so resonated with John's message that even though the location was not at all convenient, throngs of people traveled a long distance to be baptized by John.

While John baptized many people in water, he spoke consistently of one coming after him, the Messiah, who would practice a different kind of baptism. Evidently this baptism was extremely important because we read about it in all four Gospels. There aren't many events that are recorded in all four Gospels. Jesus' birth is only mentioned in two. There are a handful of miracles, such as the feeding of the 5,000 that are in all four Gospels as well as Jesus death, burial, and resurrection. This baptism that John spoke of was so critical for us to get that the Holy Spirit went out of His way to inspire all four Gospel writers to record it in their accounts of Jesus' life. Here are the four accounts:

I indeed baptize you with water unto repentance, but He who is coming after me is mightier than I, whose sandals I am not worthy to carry. He will baptize you with the Holy Spirit and fire.
—MATTHEW 3:11, NKJV

And he preached, saying, "There comes One after me who is mightier than I, whose sandal strap I am not worthy to stoop down and loose. I indeed baptized you with water, but He will baptize you with the Holy Spirit."
—MARK 1:7–8, NKJV

John answered, saying to all, "I indeed baptize you with water; but One mightier than I is coming, whose sandal strap I am not worthy to loose. He will baptize you with the Holy Spirit and fire."
—LUKE 3:16, NKJV

I did not know Him, but He who sent me to baptize with water said to me, "Upon whom you see the Spirit descending, and remaining on Him, this is He who baptizes with the Holy Spirit."
—JOHN 1:33, NKJV

All four Gospel writers repeat the same message clearly and consistently. The baptism in the Holy Spirit is not a doctrine created on an isolated scripture taken out of context or misquoted. John said this baptism was unique and something he was not capable of performing. He could only baptize people in water but he promised there is one coming, and he identified that one later as Jesus, who would baptize in the Holy Spirit and fire.

Not only did John tell us that Jesus came to baptize in the Holy Spirit, Jesus Himself was baptized in the Holy Spirit. When John baptized Jesus in water, the heavens opened up and the Holy Spirit descended on Him in bodily form like a dove and he was baptized in the Holy Spirit (John 1:32; Luke 3:22).

John recorded, "He upon whom you see the Spirit descending and remaining upon Him, he is the one who baptizes in the Holy Spirit"

(John 1:33, NKJV). Jesus was not the first person to be filled with the Holy Spirit. In the Old Testament we read of many people who did supernatural things that were beyond their own natural, human limitations when the Holy Spirit came upon them. But those fillings were always for a limited time and a specific purpose. The difference with Jesus was that He was filled with the Holy Spirit, not for a limited time but, as John said, He is the one whom the Spirit descended on and remained upon. Then for the rest of His life and ministry Jesus did miraculous things that ushered in the kingdom: things like healing the sick, raising the dead, casting out demons, calming a storm, turning water into wine, feeding the 5000, and more. He had been baptized in the Holy Spirit and the Spirit empowered Him to not just preach a message about the kingdom but to do ministry that demonstrated the kingdom. That was the source of Jesus' power for ministry. The Holy Spirit didn't just come upon Him but the Spirit remained upon Him.

In his book *Surprised by the Voice of God*, Jack Deere wrote, "At the beginning of Christ's public ministry, both Luke and Jesus Himself made it absolutely clear that the source of the power for Jesus ministry was not his deity but rather His dependence on the Holy Spirit."[1]

> Jesus returned to Galilee in the power of the Spirit, and news about him spread through the whole countryside. He was teaching in their synagogues, and everyone praised him. He went to Nazareth, where he had been brought up, and on the Sabbath day he went into the synagogue, as was his custom. And he stood up to read and the scroll of the prophet Isaiah was handed to him. Unrolling it, he found the place where it is written: "The Spirit of the Lord is on me, because he has anointed me to proclaim good news to the poor. He has sent me to proclaim freedom for the prisoners and recovery of sight for the blind, to set the oppressed free, to proclaim the year of the Lord's favor." Then he rolled up the scroll, gave it back to the attendant and sat down. The eyes of everyone in the synagogue were fastened on him. He began by saying to them, "Today this scripture is fulfilled in your hearing."
> —LUKE 4:14–21

Deere continues,

> This same testimony appears again in the middle of his ministry.
> Jesus said he cast out demons by "the Spirit of God" (Matthew
> 11:28). Matthew said on one occasion when a great crowd fol-
> lowed Jesus that "He healed all their sick" (Matthew 12:15). At first
> glance you might think Matthew attributed this healing power to
> the deity of Jesus, but just a few verses later, Matthew said that
> this fulfilled the prophecy of Isaiah, "I will put my Spirit upon
> him" (Matthew 12:18 citing Isaiah 42:1). After Jesus' resurrection
> and ascension, Peter summed up his ministry in the following
> way: God anointed Jesus of Nazareth with the Holy Spirit and
> power, and how he went around doing good and healing all who
> were under the power of the devil, because God was with him
> (Acts 10:38). This is important because John promised that Jesus
> would baptize his followers in the same Holy Spirit that Jesus was
> baptized in.[2]

Toward the end of His ministry, Jesus began to talk to the disciples
and tell them He wasn't going to be around much longer. There is a discourse recorded in John 14–16 that all takes place in the Upper Room
following what we refer to as the Last Supper. In John 13, Jesus and
His disciples arrived in the Upper Room to share the Passover meal
together and Jesus washed the disciples' feet. Jesus knew that His time
was short on the earth. He was going to be handed over to die on the
cross, be buried, rise again, and leave His disciples to carry on His
ministry in the world. During this discourse He spent time preparing
them for their ministry.

As Jesus explained that He wouldn't be with them much longer, the
disciples didn't understand. They want to know, "Why do you have to
go away Jesus? We love being with you and doing life and ministry
with you." Think through how the disciples must have felt. For three
years they had been living with, traveling with, eating with, and doing
life with Jesus. They had a front row seat as He turned water into wine,
walked on water, multiplied the loaves and fish and allowed the lame to

walk, the blind to see, the sick to be healed, and the dead raised. They were crazy in love with this guy and convinced beyond a shadow of a doubt that He was the Messiah. They wanted to be with Him forever. So, when Jesus said He was leaving and going to die soon, you can imagine that absolutely crushed them.

If you have ever been through the experience of knowing the person you love most on the earth is dying, you know it's one of the most heart-rending experiences you can ever go through. I would imagine that is exactly how the disciples were feeling at this point. Jesus, the One they loved so much, was telling them that He was going to die soon. In the midst of this time of preparation for His death, Jesus began to teach again about the Holy Spirit coming to empower the disciples after His death. In the course of this teaching, He makes what must have seemed to the disciples to be some crazy, outlandish statements. For instance, "Very truly I tell you, whoever believes in me will do the works I have been doing. He will do even greater things than these, because I am going to the Father" (John 14:12). Jesus had been informing His disciples that He was leaving. He told them they couldn't go with Him and they needed to stay and advance the kingdom. He made this amazing promise that when He was gone they would not just preach the message He had been preaching about the kingdom but they would also do the things He had been doing that demonstrated the kingdom—and even greater things!

But how would they have the power to do these greater things than Jesus did? Jesus said, "I will ask the Father, and he will give you another advocate to help you and be with you forever—the Spirit of truth" (vv. 16–17). Jesus said the way they would be empowered to do the things He had been doing and even greater things was that He was sending someone else, the Holy Spirit, to empower them to do even greater things than He had done.

This is an incredible promise that many of us have dismissed and thought surely Jesus didn't really mean we would do greater things than He did. But that phrase in the Greek that is translated "greater things" is an amazing phrase. It literally means "greater things." How would His disciples, and as Jesus said, anyone who has faith in Him, be able to do greater things than Jesus had been doing? Because Jesus was going to send another counselor, the Holy Spirit.

We use the word *another* in a couple of different ways. Let me illustrate. A few years ago I was in a car accident and my little red Saturn was totaled. Because the insurance company totaled my car, I had to get another car. I didn't get another Saturn. I got a Hyundai this time. It was another car but it was another car of *a different kind*. That is one way we use the word *another*. There is a second way we use this same word. If I had gotten another red Saturn built in the same year, it would have still been another car but it would have been another of *the same kind*.

In the original Greek, there are actually two different words for "another." One word means "another of a different kind." That's not the word used here. The word here means "another of the exact same kind." When we understand this, it is really rich. Jesus is saying to His friends, "I am leaving but I'm not leaving you alone. When I leave I will ask the Father and He will send you another counselor, of the exact same kind that I have been." It's not like Jesus is saying, "You had Me but now you have to settle for the Holy Spirit and He's okay. He's another counselor different than Me and not nearly as good or as powerful as having Me with you, but you will be okay." That's not what He said.

What Jesus literally said was, "I'm sending you another of the exact same kind; a duplicate of Me." He is not saying that the Father is going to send a lesser counselor or an inferior counselor, but rather, "When Holy Spirit comes He will be another counselor of the exact same kind that I have been. He will empower you do the same things I have done when I have been with you."

And just in case they missed what Jesus was saying, Jesus made another amazing statement: "It is to your advantage that I go away; for if I do not go away, the Helper will not come to you; but if I depart, I will send Him to you" (John 16:7, NKJV). Think about how outrageous this statement must have been to the disciples. For the past three years you have been there for all the miracles, all the healings, all the deliverances, all the raising people from the dead. Not only that, but Jesus had delegated power and authority to these guys and they had both preached the message of the kingdom and done the ministry of the kingdom. They had healed the sick and taken authority over demons. At this point they were probably thinking, "It can't get any better than being with Jesus and ministering with Jesus. This is the ultimate pinnacle." Evidently it could get better than that because Jesus just said, "It is to your advantage that I am leaving because when I go I will send Holy Spirit and you will do even greater things than I have done." Jesus was clearly saying when Holy Spirit came and they were baptized in the Spirit and fire it would be better for them than having Him there with them.

I think many believers often wonder, "What would it have been like to be with Jesus in His ministry? To see Him heal the sick, cast out demons, raise the dead, do miracles? Wow, I would love to have been there for that." But Jesus said we are better off having the Holy Spirit, because having the Spirit in us is better than having Jesus with us. Why? Because the same Holy Spirit who empowered Jesus to do signs and wonders that demonstrated the kingdom wants to fill us and overflow out of us empowering us to do the same things He did.

Just as Jesus promised, a short time later He was arrested and crucified. The disciples fled in fear of their lives. Then Jesus resurrected from the dead and spent forty days with the disciples. I think we sometimes gloss over this and have the idea that Jesus rose from the dead and appeared to the disciples just long enough to convince them He was alive; and then boom, He ascended to heaven and was gone. But for forty days He appeared to them and taught them. What did He teach during these forty days? "After his suffering, he presented himself to them and gave many convincing proofs that he was alive. He appeared to them over a period of forty days and spoke about the kingdom of God" (Acts 1:3). He taught them more about the kingdom.

Then, right before Jesus ascended into heaven, He gathered His disciples together for some final instruction. It is recorded for us in Acts

1. Now I've got to tell you, if someone rises from the dead to say something we ought to pay attention, don't you think?

> On one occasion, while he was eating with them, he gave them this command: "Do not leave Jerusalem, but wait for the gift my Father promised, which you have heard me speak about. For John baptized with water, but in a few days you will be baptized with the Holy Spirit."
>
> —Acts 1:4–5

John had baptized in water but he promised that when Jesus came He was going to baptize with the Holy Spirit. Jesus told the disciples you need that! Evidently these guys had not experienced Spirit baptism yet. And Jesus had instructed them previously that it wouldn't happen until He returned to the Father. And now He was saying He was about ready to go the Father and they would soon be baptized in the Holy Spirit.

There is an intriguing passage in John 20:22. Following Jesus' resurrection it says, "And with that he breathed on them and said, 'Receive the Holy Spirit.'" After His resurrection Jesus breathed on the disciples and told them to receive the Holy Spirit and then after spending the next month teaching them about the kingdom, he told them they needed to go and wait for the baptism of the Holy Spirit. Evidently this was something different that was going to happen to them.

I believe when Jesus breathed on the disciples and told them to receive the Holy Spirit this was the point of their conversion. They had seen the risen Christ, who had died to pay for their sins, and they put their complete faith in Him and so they received the Holy Spirit. Make no mistake about it, there is no conversion, no new birth, apart from the Holy Spirit infusing our dead spirit and making us alive again. We cannot be converted and become a Christian without the Holy Spirit regenerating our heart. But there is something else, something different, something more. Jesus told the disciples to go and wait for it in Jerusalem. It was the baptism in the Holy Spirit. What was going to happen when the Holy Spirit came on them?

> But you will receive power when the Holy Spirit comes on you; and you will be my witnesses in Jerusalem, and in all Judea and Samaria, and to the ends of the earth.
>
> —ACTS 1:8

Jesus was saying in effect, "I am getting ready to leave and return to heaven. As the Father sent Me, so send I you. My assignment to destroy the works of the devil is now your assignment. You are to go out and preach the message of the kingdom and do the ministry that demonstrates the kingdom, but you are not ready yet. You have the assignment but you haven't been empowered yet to fulfill the assignment. Because even though the Holy Spirit came *in* you at conversion, He has to come *on* you to prepare you for ministry. You need to be baptized in the Holy Spirit." Bill Johnson puts it this way: "He is in me for my sake, but He's upon me for yours." At conversion the Holy Spirit comes in us to begin to transform us, but when we are baptized in the Spirit, He comes on us in power for the benefit of others."[3] You will receive power when the Holy Spirit comes on you. And Jesus is clear that His followers need that!

So put yourself in the place of these disciples. Jesus has just told you to go and wait for the baptism in the Holy Spirit and when that happens you will receive some serious power. He said, "Don't go out and try to be my witnesses without that power." 'Wait," you think. "What is this going to look like? We're going to be baptized in the Holy Spirit and it will be better than having Jesus here with us? We're going to have power to be witnesses to the whole world?" They were just waiting and waiting in that Upper Room, and then it happened.

> When the day of Pentecost came, they were all together in one place. Suddenly a sound like the blowing of a violent wind came from heaven and filled the whole house where they were sitting. They saw what seemed to be tongues of fire that separated and

came to rest on each of them. All of them were filled with the Holy Spirit and began to speak in other tongues as the Spirit enabled them.

—ACTS 2:1–4

Put yourself in that Upper Room for a moment. You know Jesus has promised you would be baptized in the Holy Spirit. And so you're there and you're waiting and you're praying, and then all of a sudden you hear this intense noise that sounds like a hurricane rushing through the room. Then you see tongues of fire come and sit on people's heads and everyone starts speaking in languages they don't know. I don't think they wondered, "Is this it? Is this what Jesus was talking about?" They knew beyond a shadow of a doubt this was it! They knew they had been baptized in the Holy Spirit. And just as Jesus promised, they received power to continue to advance the kingdom by both preaching the message Jesus preached and doing the ministry He did.

Now there were staying in Jerusalem God-fearing Jews from every nation under heaven. When they heard this sound, a crowd came together in bewilderment, because each one heard their own language being spoken. Utterly amazed, they asked: "Are not all these who are speaking Galileans? Then how is it that each of us hears them in our native language?

—ACTS 2:5–8

The Holy Spirit came and baptized the disciples and others who were in that Upper Room, and there was a huge crowd gathered in Jerusalem from all over the world to celebrate the feast of Pentecost. These people from different nations spoke many different languages, but all of a sudden they started hearing these Galileans speaking in their own native language.

One might have said, "I understand that. I hear them speaking Arabic." Another, "Mama mia! That's Italian!" Someone else, "Wait! That was Chinese." All these people were gathered from all different regions of the world and spoke different languages, and yet miraculously they all heard the message being shared in their own language. They must have been confused as to what all this could possibly mean. It wasn't natural. It was supernatural. Now that's the Holy Spirit! When something happens and you know there is no way for it to be happening by natural means, only supernatural, that's the Holy Spirit. The Holy Spirit's power is not something that can be mimicked. You can't look at something the Holy Spirit does and say, "I can do that." When Jesus baptized these early followers in the Holy Spirit, there was an incredible power evidenced that caused the others who saw what was transpiring to be bewildered and amazed and ask, 'What is this?"

"Some, however, made fun of them and said, 'They have had too much wine'" (Acts 2:13). Evidently there was something so out of the ordinary about the way these people were acting that some thought they were drunk. But they were not drunk with wine. It was way too early in the day for that to be happening! They were drunk with the Holy Spirit. They were out of control because they were under the supernatural control of the Spirit of God.

> Then Peter stood up with the Eleven, raised his voice and addressed the crowd: "Fellow Jews and all of you who live in Jerusalem, let me explain this to you; listen carefully to what I say. These men are not drunk, as you suppose. It's only nine in the morning! No, this is what was spoken by the prophet Joel:
>
> 'In the last days, God says, I will pour out my Spirit on all people. Your sons and daughters will prophesy, your young men will see visions, your old men will dream dreams. Even on my servants, both men and women, I will pour out my Spirit in those days, and they will prophesy. I will show wonders in the heaven above and signs on the earth below, blood and fire and billows of smoke. The sun will be turned to darkness and the moon to blood before the coming of the great and glorious day of the Lord. And everyone who calls on the name of the Lord will be saved.'"
>
> —Acts 2:14–21

In Old Testament times, God would occasionally pour out His Spirit on specific people for specific purposes and for a limited time. Usually the Spirit would come upon prophets, priests, and kings. When the Spirit would come upon them they would prophesy, they would dream dreams, they would have incredible power of some kind; but the filling was only temporary and then the Spirit would leave. In the last days, which began at Pentecost and continues to this day, God said "I will pour out my Spirit on all men." Not just prophets and priests and kings will have the Holy Spirit and not just for specific times and purposes; but He will come upon all men and women, old and young, and they will prophesy, dream dreams, speak in tongues, heal the sick, cast out demons, and raise the dead because the Holy Spirit has come upon them and they have been baptized in Holy Spirit and fire.

After this experience Peter preached an incredible sermon about how Jesus was the Son of God who had been crucified but God raised Him from the dead. He wrapped up his message with these words:

> "Therefore let all Israel be assured of this: God has made this Jesus, whom you crucified, both Lord and Messiah." When the people heard this, they were cut to the heart and said to Peter and the other apostles, "Brothers, what shall we do?" Peter replied, "Repent and be baptized, every one of you, in the name of Jesus Christ for the forgiveness of your sins. And you will receive the gift of the Holy Spirit. The promise is for you and your children and for all who are far off—for all whom the Lord our God will call."
>
> —ACTS 2:36–39

This promise of the baptism of the Holy Spirit was not just for the disciples but they promised it was for everyone else gathered there that day and for all believers from that day forward. Peter said it was for their children and their children's children and all who were far off. He's saying, "Do you see what is going on here? Do you see this power of the Spirit displayed? It can be yours."

As we look at the church in the Book of Acts, we see this baptism in the Holy Spirit allowed the followers of Jesus to fulfill their assignment to destroy the works of the devil. The primary message they preached was the same message they had learned from Jesus. It was the message of the kingdom.

> But when they believed Philip as he proclaimed the good news of the kingdom of God and the name of Jesus Christ, they were baptized, both men and women.
>
> —Acts 8:12

> Paul entered the synagogue and spoke boldly there for three months, arguing persuasively about the kingdom of God.
>
> —Acts 19:8

> He proclaimed the kingdom of God and taught about the Lord Jesus Christ—with all boldness and without hindrance!
>
> —Acts 28:31

But they not only preached the message about the kingdom, they demonstrated the reality that the kingdom had come through the ministry they did. Just a quick sampling of the next chapters clearly shows how the works of the kingdom were predominant in the ministry of the early church.

In Acts 3, we read about Peter and John going to the temple to pray. On their way they encountered a lame man begging outside the temple. He wanted money. They told him they had no money but what they did have they would freely give Him. They told him to rise and walk! And he did. Where did they get the power to do that? They had been baptized in the Holy Spirit.

In chapter 4 they asked God to stretch out his hand and heal and perform miraculous signs and wonders in the name of Jesus (v. 30). After they prayed, the place where they were all meeting was shaken and they were filled with the Holy Spirit and spoke the word of God boldly (v. 31). It was evidence of the baptism in the Holy Spirit.

In chapter 5 Ananias and Sapphira lied about giving all the proceeds from the sale of their property to the church. Peter said they lied to the Holy Spirit and they both dropped dead (vv. 1–11). The next verses read,

> The apostles performed many miraculous signs and wonders among the people. And all the believers used to meet together in Solomon's Colonnade. No one else dared join them, even though they were highly regarded by the people. Nevertheless, more and more men and women believed in the Lord and were added to their number. As a result, people brought the sick into the streets and laid them on beds and mats so that at least Peter's shadow might fall on some of them as he passed by. Crowds gathered also from the towns around Jerusalem, bringing their sick and those tormented by impure spirits, and all of them were healed.
>
> —Acts 5:12–16

Notice they did the ministry that demonstrated the kingdom. The same ministry Jesus did. They cast out demons and healed the sick. How? They were empowered by the baptism in the Holy Spirit.

In chapter 6 Stephen was preaching and doing miraculous signs and wonders among the people and they arrested him.

In chapter 8 Philip, an evangelist, not only preached the message of the kingdom but did miraculous signs that demonstrated the kingdom and the people paid close attention to Him (vv 4–8). He was casting out evil spirits and the sick were being healed. In Samaria, the apostles laid their hands on new believers who received the baptism in the Holy Spirit (vv. 14–17). They needed that to preach the message of the kingdom and do the ministry of the kingdom.

Also in chapter 8 Philip had a word of knowledge about a eunuch from Ethiopia and he went and shared the good news with him (vv. 26–35).

In chapter 9, by the power of the Holy Spirit, Peter raised a woman from the dead (vv. 36–41).

In chapter 10 Peter had a vision and went to Cornelius' house and preached (vv. 9–43).

> While Peter was still speaking these words, the Holy Spirit came
> on all who heard the message. The circumcised believers who had
> come with Peter were astonished that the gift of the Holy Spirit
> had been poured out even on the Gentiles. For they heard them
> speaking in tongues and praising God. Then Peter said, "Surely
> no one can stand in the way of their being baptized with water?
> They have received the Holy Spirit just as we have."
>
> —ACTS 10:44-46

In chapter 11 Agabus went to Paul and prophesied about future
events (v. 28).

In chapter 12 the church gathered to pray for Peter who had been
thrown in prison. Miraculously, an angel came and freed him from
prison and Peter showed up at their prayer meeting (vv. 1–18).

In chapter 13 Paul met up with a sorcerer and told him he was a
child of the devil. He prophesied that the man would go blind and it
happened, so more people put their faith in Jesus (vv. 6–12).

In chapter 14 another lame man was healed (vv. 8–10). I think you
get the point. They were preaching the message of the kingdom and
doing the ministry of the kingdom. Jesus had promised them, "You
will receive power when the Holy Spirit comes on you and you will
be my witnesses" and that is exactly what happened. When people are
baptized in the Holy Spirit, He comes upon them in power and signs
and wonders follow.

I heard someone say one time, "I'm not sure we should expect miracles. Miracles shouldn't be ordinary." Yet when we look at the early
church, we see over and over again that when people were baptized
in the Holy Spirit, power followed that allowed them to perform signs
and wonders demonstrating the message of the kingdom. The power
to operate in the kingdom is found in the baptism in the Holy Spirit.
That's the power He wants to bring into our lives to allow us to be His
witnesses.

The same thing is true today. The kingdom is still both a message
and a ministry. In most churches today we have ignored the gospel

of the kingdom and instead have preached a gospel of salvation. We have simply preached Jesus as Savior who forgives our sins and makes it possible for us to go to heaven someday, but we have missed Jesus as Lord who empowers people to live and operate in kingdom power today.

But the kingdom is not just a message. It is a ministry. Ministry in most churches looks like programs and classes and it's all pretty institutional. It doesn't look anything like the ministry of the kingdom we see in the New Testament church.

In my conservative church background and training, I was taught a whole lot more about what the Holy Spirit doesn't do today than what He does do. For years I would read these things in the Book of Acts and the way the Holy Spirit empowered those early believers to do the same things Jesus did that demonstrated the reality of the kingdom and I would wonder deep down inside, "Am I missing something? Is there more? There has to be more." Finally I came to the point where I was tired of talking about what the Holy Spirit did in the past and doesn't do today and decided I was going to start trusting the Holy Spirit—the same Holy Spirit who raised Jesus from dead, the same Holy Spirit who empowered Jesus to demonstrate the kingdom, the same Holy Spirit who empowered that early church—to empower me to advance the kingdom of God and take authority over the works of the devil. And I found there really is so much more!

Much of what is happening in American churches today makes sense with or without the help of the Holy Spirit. Here's what I mean. I believe that I have been given leadership gifts which have allowed me to be successful in leading a church, but I also believe that some of the same leadership abilities I've been given would allow me to be successful in leading in the marketplace. I believe I could lead a business and be pretty successful using a lot of the same leadership abilities I use in the church. But when I see what happens when the Holy Spirit takes over a church and His power consumes the life of an individual, it goes way beyond talent or natural abilities. When the baptism of the Holy Spirit comes upon a person, things happen that can only be explained by the power of the Holy Spirit. Things start to happen that cannot be mimicked, faked, or explained on the basis of raw talent or human ability. When the Holy Spirit comes into the life of a person and He empowers them, the evidence of that is signs and wonders that demonstrate the kingdom.

Sometimes we go to one of two extremes in churches. Some fundamental, conservative evangelical churches want to deny the power of the Holy Spirit exists today because of a lack of personal experience. So they have developed a teaching to validate their lack of experience by saying the supernatural gifts of the Spirit died out with the apostles. But Jesus didn't say His followers would receive power when the Holy Spirit comes on them for just a limited period of time. In fact, Peter made it clear on Pentecost this promise was for all generations.

On the other hand, many charismatic churches believe in the power of the Spirit to do miraculous things today yet they want to use that power to have a private party every weekend at church. Jesus didn't say we would receive power to build ourselves up when the Holy Spirit comes on us. He said we would receive power when the Holy Spirit came upon us to be His witnesses. What is amazing is that when you think through almost all the miraculous signs and wonders that were done by the apostles and others empowered by the Holy Spirit and recorded in Acts, almost none of these healings or resurrections or deliverances were done in a church service. Why? Because the power was given to be witnesses, to demonstrate God's power to those who do not yet believe.

When we preach the message of the kingdom without a demonstration of the kingdom, it just reduces it to another good idea, another philosophy, another set of values and ideals that can be compared to any other philosophy. But when we preach the message of the kingdom along with a demonstration of the kingdom, with signs and wonders and healing and deliverance, that demonstration of the power of God produces the desired effect—people come to God. That's the kingdom. It is a spontaneous, Spirit-inspired, empowered, presentation of the gospel.

Jesus said, "You will receive power when the Holy Spirit comes upon you and you will be my witnesses." When you think of the kingdom mission Jesus has assigned to us, why would He not want to empower us with the same Holy Spirit—the same power that anointed Jesus, the same power that Jesus told His disciples they needed before they were ready to advance the kingdom, and the same power that He said would allow His followers to do the same things and even greater things than He did? Why would He not want to give you and me that same power to advance His kingdom? The truth is, not only does He desire to give it to us, we too, just like the apostles, cannot really be effective in fulfilling our assignment without it. The promise that you will receive power when the Holy Spirit comes on you was not just for the apostles and the early church but for you and your children and your children's children.

Maybe you received the Holy Spirit when you believed and think that is all there is. However, as we have already seen, the disciples had already received the Holy Spirit but they hadn't been baptized in the Holy Spirit.

Let me give you another example that clearly shows that these are two separate events. In Acts 8 there is an incredible evangelist by the name of Philip who was preaching both the message of the kingdom and doing the ministry of kingdom in Samaria and a huge revival broke out. People were coming to Jesus left and right. It was a beautiful thing.

> When the apostles in Jerusalem heard that Samaria had accepted the word of God, they sent Peter and John to them. When they arrived, they prayed for the new believers there that they might receive the Holy Spirit, because the Holy Spirit had not yet come on any of them; they had simply been baptized in name of the Lord Jesus. Then Peter and John placed their hands on them, and they received the Holy Spirit.
>
> —ACTS 8:14–17

Notice these people in Samaria had trusted Jesus for salvation and been baptized in water. They were saved. However, they had not yet been baptized in the Holy Spirit. The Holy Spirit had not yet fallen on any of them. Then the apostles came and laid their hands on them and they received the baptism of the Holy Spirit. Conversion and the baptism of the Holy Spirit were two separate and distinct events. Just because we have trusted Jesus for salvation does not mean we have received the baptism of the Holy Spirit for power. But I have good news! Jesus still baptizes people in the Holy Spirit today.

Our assignment has not changed. We too are called to "heal the sick, cleanse the lepers, raise the dead, cast out demons. Freely you have received, freely give" (Matt. 10:8, NKJV). Just as Jesus needed the power of the baptism of the Holy Spirit to destroy the works of the devil and He then instructed His disciples that they were not ready to perform kingdom ministry until they received Holy Spirit baptism, we too need Holy Spirit baptism. This baptism of fire changes everything!

How do you receive the baptism of the Holy Spirit? The same way you received salvation. You ask for it by faith.

> Which of you fathers, if your son asks for a fish, will give him a snake instead? Or if he asks for an egg, will give him a scorpion? If you then, though you are evil, know how to give good gifts to your children, how much more will your Father in heaven give the Holy Spirit to those who ask him!
>
> —LUKE 11:11–13

Chapter 9

IDENTITY CRISIS

ONE OF THE clearer memories I have from childhood is of my mother praying with me almost every day before I left for school. Talk about putting a wet blanket on any sinful plans I had for the day! Then before I would walk out the door, she often said this, "Remember who you are and remember whose you are." It is absolutely critical that those of us who are called to do the ministry of the kingdom know who we are and whose we are.

When we are born again, we are born into the kingdom of God. And when that new birth occurs, when God infuses our dead spirit and brings about this new birth, we are instantly in His kingdom and we are given a message to preach—the message of the kingdom. In this kingdom the King Himself gives us a ministry to carry out. It is the same ministry that Jesus performed. It is the ministry that demonstrates that the kingdom is here.

But if it is true that we have been given the power of the Holy Spirit and been delegated authority from the King to go out and take dominion by advancing His kingdom, why is it that so many believers still live as though they are afraid of the demonic? Why do so many believers feel unworthy to ask for healing or blessing or anything else from the King? Why are so many believers simply content to receive salvation but never fulfill their assignment to advance the kingdom? I believe it's because we don't really know who we are and we don't really know whose we are. We don't understand our identity in the kingdom.

In Luke 15:11–32 Jesus told one of his most famous parables. It's a story that most of us have read or at least heard at one time or another. It's the story of the prodigal son. This story can help us get our arms around the truth of our identity and the difference that embracing our identity can make when it comes to advancing the kingdom.

The story begins with the younger of two sons deciding it was time for him to leave home. Maybe he was tired of Dad's rules. Maybe he wanted to see the world or prove that he could make it on his own. But whatever his reasoning, this son approached his father one day and made a request of him. He said, "Dad, I would like you to give me my share of the inheritance." Now this was a shocking request that revealed that this boy had a complete lack of respect for his father. You see, in the Jewish culture of Jesus' day, it was absolutely unheard of for a son to go to his father and ask for his share of the inheritance. The father was the one who would decide the right timing to give the inheritance to his son. But this boy disrespectfully asked the father to give him his share of the inheritance.

It was also the custom of that culture that when the inheritance was given a respectful son would never think to take that inheritance and use it selfishly to make his own way in the world. He would use the money, first of all, to stay home and take care of his parents until the day they died. But that was not the case with this son. He wanted his father's money but not his father's rules, and so he went to his father and asked for his portion of the inheritance. What's even more amazing is that the father granted his son's request. He gave the boy his inheritance. I can picture this father watching his son leave home with his pocket's jingling. There were most likely tears in his father's eyes because his heart was broken, but he let the boy go. He didn't try to stop him.

What did the boy do with his newly acquired funds? As Jesus tells the story, He said the boy wasted his father's money on wild living. We don't know for sure what that included, but I think we have a pretty good idea. Perhaps drugs, parties, drunken binges, prostitutes, or maybe he gambled it away. All those would be things that we would refer to as wild living. And while we don't know exactly what the wild living was, we do know that he blew all the money that his father had given him. This money took his father a lifetime to accumulate but the prodigal wasted it all in a short period of time.

All of a sudden the boy found himself homeless and broke. He was in desperate shape. But as desperate as he was, things were about to go from bad to worse because the next thing that Jesus told us was that there was a severe famine in the land and the boy got pretty hungry. It's bad enough to be broke, but to be broke during a famine is really bad because there is no way to live off the fat of the land and survive.

Now what could he do? He knew what he couldn't do. He could never go back to his father's house. So he jumped on Craigslist and searched for local job opportunities. He could only find one: working for a pig farmer slopping pigs. If you know anything about the Jewish people, you know they would have nothing to do with pigs. Pigs were considered unclean animals. Jesus was telling this story that day to a group of Jewish religious leaders. I picture them squirming in their seats because when ,Jesus said, this boy went to work for a pig farmer slopping pigs there was absolutely nothing Jesus could have said to make this boy more despicable in the eyes of his Jewish father than this.

The boy was so desperate when he took this job that, Jesus said, even the pods that the pigs were eating looked good to him. Now that's desperate! When the pig's food starts to look good, you know you have hit rock bottom.

So here the boy is knee-deep in pig slop and, Jesus said, he came to his senses and began to dream about life back home. He thought about the servants in his father's house and how they got three square meals a day and they had a bed to sleep in and a roof over their heads. He knew his dad would never take him back as a son, but he wondered if perhaps he would take him back as a servant.

He began to rehearse a speech. "Father, I have sinned against heaven and against you. I am no longer worthy to be called your son, just take me back as one of your hired men." After rehearsing the speech and getting it down pat, he apprehensively started back to his father's house. What would his father think? What was he going to say? How was he going to explain how he had wasted his entire inheritance? Would his father even speak to him?

Much to the son's amazement, as he got within a few hundred yards of home, his father came running out to meet him. He hadn't even hit the driveway yet; but as he got close enough to be seen, his father, who had been watching and waiting for this moment when his son would come home, ran out to meet him.

The boy started to recite his speech, "Father, I have sinned against heaven and against you I am no longer worthy to be called your son" (v. 21). But the boy couldn't even get the words out of his mouth. His dad didn't want to hear any more of this nonsense about no longer being worthy to he called his son. He shouted to his servants to quickly bring the best robe and put it on his son. He told them to put a ring on his finger and sandals on his feet. He said to get the biggest, fattest calf they had and slaughter it because it was party time! The son who was dead was alive again. He was lost but now found (vv. 22–24).

Most of us know that in this story the father represents God. He is the King of the kingdom. And the prodigals are every one of us who, like Adam and Eve in the garden, have rebelled against the King's authority and said, "I don't want to live in Your kingdom any longer. I want to go out and build my own kingdom."

At some point along the way, many of us have come to our senses and have come to the conclusion that building our own kingdom was not at all what we thought it would be. We decided to go back home, back to the King's palace to live under His rule and reign and experience His benefits. When we went back home we found that we have an incredibly gracious King who accepts us and takes us back and even celebrates our return.

But here's what I think we so often miss. We miss the identity He gives us. We forget who we are and whose we are. Notice that when this prodigal came home, he simply asked the father to give him what he thought he might be able to earn. He simply requested a place as a servant living in the servant's quarters. He wasn't looking for anything more than that. But the father would have no part of that. He pretty much even ignored the request and paid no attention to his talk about being a servant. He didn't even let him finish his speech. He interrupted him and said, "You will never be my servant. You are my son. Hey get the ring and put it his on finger, the robe on his back and sandals on his feet. Get the fattest calf we have and kill it because we are going to have a party! My son was dead and he is alive again!"

Pay attention to the items listed in verse 22 that the father placed on his son, because each individual item contains priceless and profound insight into our Father's love for those of us who would bear the title of son or daughter. The father instructed them to "Bring the best robe and put it on him." In placing the best robe on the boy, the father was telling the prodigal that his position as son was being restored. It was an immediate demonstration of complete acceptance, love, and approval. All of the major benefits of being his son were being restored.

Then the father said, "Put a ring on his finger." A ring was not only a sign of great affection but it was also a symbol of authority. Pharaoh removed his signet ring and put it on Joseph's finger when installing him into a position of leadership in Egypt (Gen. 41:42). In the Book of Esther, the king took off his royal signet ring by which the decrees of his government were signed and gave it Mordecai (Esther 8:2). The rings symbolically transferred to Joseph and Mordecai all the power and authority necessary for the promotions they received. The ring placed on the hand of the prodigal son indicated also a transfer of inheritance that would ordinarily have gone to the firstborn.

Then he said to put "sandals on his feet." The prodigal returned home without shoes, a sign of having become extremely destitute; in ancient biblical times only servants and slaves went barefoot. Therefore, when the father ordered shoes to be brought out and put on his son's feet, he was declaring once again that the prodigal was not to be treated as a servant but as a son with all the right and privileges that went along with that position.

Every single one of us who has ever been born again and has been born into His kingdom is a prodigal son or daughter who has come home. When we enter His kingdom, the King does not simply accept us as servants. We are adopted as sons and daughters of the King. We are not paupers living in the servant's quarters. We are adopted as princes and princesses with all the rights and privileges that come with being a son or daughter of the King. We receive the inheritance of our older brother Jesus with all the rights and privileges He has in the kingdom.

Why is this so important for us to understand? Because if we view ourselves as servants, we will only relate to the King as a servant would relate to the King, with fear and trembling. We won't ask for much. We won't expect much, because we think we are simply lucky to be in the palace at all. We will dream but we won't ask because servants don't do that.

When I was a teenager and I wanted to borrow the family car or I wanted to have some money to go out with my friends, I had no problem asking my father. I didn't always get the car and I didn't always get the money, but I wasn't afraid to ask because I was a son. I had my father's name, and I had no problem asking my father to bless me with whatever I needed. Now let me tell you what I never did. I never went to my friend's dad and asked for the keys to his car or money from his wallet, because in his family I was not a son.

When we start talking about living in the kingdom, about taking power and authority over demons, about healing the sick and cleansing lepers and raising the dead, about expecting signs and wonders and miracles to follow our ministry, if we don't see ourselves as sons and daughters of the King, then we won't ask for much. We won't expect much, and we won't be much of a threat to Satan's kingdom.

So many believers are facing an identity crisis. They are like this prodigal. They believe they have gone too far and done too much. They believe they have brought shame to the King's name. They think, "I am just lucky to be forgiven at all, let alone be a son or daughter of the King. Just let me be a servant living in the servant's quarters."

The church today is full of people who operate like servants. Too many Christians see their identity more as orphans who have to earn favor with their Father than sons or daughters who already have everything that belongs to the Father. They don't know who they are. The result is they spend time and energy trying to earn a position in the Father's house that is already theirs.

But our King says, "No way! I don't want any talk about being a servant. You are My precious son. You are my precious daughter. You are a prince or princess in My kingdom and I want you to rule and reign and take dominion over the enemy as you advance My kingdom." When we get our arms around our identity, it changes everything about how we function in the kingdom.

Look at some verses that remind us we are sons and daughters and not slaves.

> Yet to all who did receive him, to those who believed in his name, he gave the right to become children of God.
>
> —John 1:12

> What great love the Father has lavished on us, that we should be called children of God! And that is what we are!
>
> —1 John 3:1

> The Spirit you received does not make you slaves, so that you live in fear again; rather, the Spirit you received brought about your adoption to sonship. And by him we cry, "Abba, Father."
>
> —Romans 8:15

Do you understand who you are? You and I are sons and daughters of the King. We have been adopted into His royal family and have been delegated His authority. That is not just a warm fuzzy. We have been given His name. He has put the robe upon our back. He has put the signet ring of authority on our finger. He has placed sandals on our feet.

Do you understand when He wakes up in the morning you are His happy thought? He doesn't just love you; He *likes* you. Most of us have heard that He loves us. The problem is we don't feel very loved. But the truth is, if you are born again into His kingdom, you have been adopted into His family and you are His son or daughter and everything He has belongs to you.

Our family has learned something about adoption by personal experience. About eleven years ago, God clearly revealed to us that we were called to adopt a little girl from China. We already had four biological sons but God laid it on my wife, Tricia's, heart that we were to adopt a girl from China.

Even before our last two biological sons, Adam and Joshua, were born, Tricia started talking to me how she had read and heard stories about how people in China were only allowed to have one child and that most wanted that to be a boy because in their culture boys stayed home and took care of the parents in their old age. Thus, there were orphanages in China full of girls waiting for homes.

When she first brought up the idea I wasn't too excited. After we had four sons when I really only wanted to have two, I was sure that I was not interested. But Tricia did not ever give up on the idea.

Then I did something very dangerous. I agreed to pray about it and ask God whether or not it was His will for us to adopt. What I really was doing was telling my wife I would agree to pray about it to just get her off my back! But I didn't want to be disingenuous, so I really did pray.

Almost immediately we began to get "signs" indicating to us that perhaps this was something God was calling us to do. Shortly after I started praying about this, we received a chess set in the mail that we had ordered as a Christmas gift for our oldest son. It came from somewhere in Texas. When we opened the box, we discovered a beautiful Chinese fan lying on top of the chess set. There was no rhyme or reason as to why it was in there. Tricia said, "That is our sign!" I said, "No way! It's just a coincidence."

A few days later, Tricia was driving and praying about the whole idea of adoption when a song, "More Than Anything," came on with these words: "God loves people more than anything." And the last line of the song was, "More than anything he wants us to go." She started crying, feeling that God was speaking to her about going to China and adopting a daughter. I again said, "That's a coincidence."

A couple of days later in her prayer time, Tricia prayed that God would give her a sign that very day of His will regarding the adoption. Immediately after she finished that prayer, she went to a friend's house for breakfast. When she walked in and sat down at the kitchen table, she noticed her friend had a Scripture calendar. The heading for that day on the calendar in big bold letters was the word *ADOPTION*, and the verse below it was Romans 8:23: "Not only so, but we ourselves, who have the firstfruits of the Spirit, groan inwardly as we wait eagerly for our adoption to sonship." She saw that and started laughing, feeling God had given her another sign. Of course, I again said it was just coincidence; but had to admit I was starting to wonder.

That night we went over to the home of some friends who had adopted from China just to investigate what was even involved in the process. As the discussion turned to the cost, I immediately responded, "Well, there's our answer to prayer! There is no way we can afford that." And then I said, "God would have to speak to me out of a burning bush to get me to do that."

The next morning I was reading out of my *Daily Walk* devotional Bible. For some reason I was a day behind so I decided to catch up. The section I read was about how Moses had been adopted by Pharaoh's family and that God had protected him because He had a plan for Moses. That seemed like another coincidence. I started thinking about that and praying. As I prayed I said, "God, you know we can't afford this." Then God pointed out something to me. The day before, kind of out of the blue, I had pulled into a car dealership and looked at trading my car in on a minivan. I found one I really liked and had taken it to show Tricia. She liked it and we agreed to try to work out a deal. The end result was I wanted to do it but she thought we would be raising our payment too much so we agreed to pray for a day about it. We had learned the night before from our friends that adopting from China would probably cost us around $10,000 after the tax credit for adoption. I had said that it wasn't possible for us. But as I prayed that day God pointed out to me that the difference between what I owed on my car and what that minivan would cost was $10,000; I felt as though God was speaking to me saying, "You would spend $10,000 for a vehicle but not $10,000 to give a child a family?" I started to pay attention at that point.

The actual reading for that Saturday morning, the day after I had stated that God would have to speak to me from a burning bush was, as you've probably guessed, on Moses and the burning bush!

The next day, Sunday morning, I woke in the middle of the night and felt God was leading me to do a search on my computer Bible about how God feels about orphans. I found several verses about how He cares for them and how pure religion is to care for them (James 1:27).

The next night, Sunday night, I again woke up in the middle of the night and couldn't sleep. I kept feeling like God was telling me to read this book that a guy in our church had given me a couple of weeks before that. I didn't know anything about the book but I knew I didn't feel like reading, so I messed around on the computer and watched some television; but I couldn't stop thinking about the book. So finally about 4:00 a.m., I picked up the book. I had no idea what it was about but a friend had asked me to read it because he said this guy, Randy Alcorn, was his favorite author. The book was titled *Safely Home*.

As I began to read the book, I preceded to find out that it was a fic-titious story based on true facts about Christians being persecuted in

China; no other country, just China. I couldn't believe it. I woke Tricia up and told her and she laughed.

Monday morning I went to the office at church and looked through our weekly communication cards that people turn in at services on Sunday. A woman I barely even know wrote on the back of her card, "Pastor, would you please preach a sermon sometime soon on how God cares for orphans." I couldn't believe it! No one has ever asked me to preach on orphans before.

I might be dumb but I'm not stupid! Some may wonder whether or not the King still speaks today, but I can assure you from this and other personal experiences He undoubtedly speaks in real and personal ways. Through this process God had convinced me of His heart for orphans and placed a love inside of me for a little girl I had not yet even met.

There was still much to be done. We had to locate an adoption agency, go through a home study, fill out all the dossier requirements, and wait for approval. All of this took about thirteen months, and then finally we were cleared to go adopt our daughter. We traveled to China and came home with our baby girl.

Through this process, I learned a couple of things about adoption. When a child is adopted, that child takes on the family name. When we are born again, when we place our faith in Jesus, God adopts us as sons and daughters into His family. One thing that means for us is that we take on His family name and people ought to see a family resemblance in us.

Since our daughter had been abandoned and was in an orphanage, she had no family name, no identity. When we adopted her into our family, we gave her our name. Her name at the orphanage in China was simply Yi Bei which literally meant "baby from Yi-Xing." It was the village in which she had been born and abandoned. But when we adopted her, we gave her a new name. She is now Rachel Yi Bei Hudson. She took our family name.

When our King adopts us, He calls us His sons and daughters. We are princes and princesses in His kingdom and people ought to recognize us as children of the King.

Matthew 25:14–30 records a story Jesus told about a master who went away on a journey and entrusted some of his money to his servants to use. Some used the master's money well and multiplied it. One buried it in the ground. When the master returned home, he had commended those who had used his money well with the words, "Well done, good and faithful servant....Enter into the joy of your master" (vv. 21, 23, NAS). Many of us quote those words as words we hope to hear from God one day. I sure want to hear those from God, but I'm really looking for more. I want to watch Him throw His arms around me and put the robe on my back and the ring on my finger and say, "Welcome home, son. You remind me a whole lot of your older brother Jesus."

I heard a story of a middle-aged woman who had a serious heart attack and ended up in the hospital. She thought she was going to die so she asked the Lord, "Is it my time to go?" God said, "No. You have forty-three more years, eight more months, and ten more days to live." She thought, "Wow! I have way more time left than I thought and I'm getting some mileage on me. Maybe I should get some work done while I'm here in the hospital." So she got a tummy tuck, liposuction, a facelift, and even had her hair colored. It was one of those extreme makeovers. When she was released, she was crossing the street and got run over by a car and died. When she got to heaven she was confused; she asked God, "I thought You said I had forty-three more years left to live. Why didn't You protect me?" God replied, "I didn't recognize you!"

We have to ask ourselves if we are living up to the family name. Are we living as a son or daughter of the King? Would people see the resemblance between us and our older brother Jesus? Are we preaching the message He preached, the message of the kingdom, and doing the works He did, the ministry of the kingdom?

Another thing adoption does is give the adoptee an equal share in the family inheritance. When we adopted Rachel into our family, she received all the same benefits as our four biological sons. Her right to any inheritance will be the same as theirs because she is our child. When God adopted us into His family, He not only gave us the family name, He also included us in the family inheritance. We are joint heirs with Jesus. God has given us all the inheritance of His kingdom. All the riches of His kingdom are ours, both now and in the future. We are given full rights and privileges as sons and daughters of the King. As we talk about moving in power and authority; taking dominion over demons; destroying the works of the devil; moving in signs, wonders, and miracles; and healing the sick, raising the dead, and other acts that demonstrate the kingdom has come, what I find is that a lot of people are afraid to ask or to at least ask expectantly and not reluctantly because they don't know who they are and they don't know whose we are.

Many of us are fighting for something we already have. We're fighting for acceptance from our Dad when we have already been accepted. There is nothing we can do to make ourselves more acceptable to our King than we already are. When Jesus said on the cross, "It is finished" (John 19:30), He really meant it. There is nothing more we can do to become more acceptable or walk in more power and authority. He did all there was to do. I believe that most of the church is fighting for acceptance and sonship when in reality we can't fight for something we already have. Instead of fighting for sonship, we need to learn to fight from sonship. A lot of the reason we don't expect much from the King is because the enemy has convinced us that we are not worthy, that we are not sons and daughters of the King but rather we are simply slaves. If we see ourselves as slaves, we feel like we have to achieve and earn our spot to be in the kingdom. Nothing in the kingdom can be achieved by us, whether salvation, healing, authority over demons, or spiritual gifts. None of it can be achieved. It can only be received. When we recognize our identity as sons or daughters of the King, we learn to become good receivers.

In Jack Frost's teaching on sonship, he points out some key differences between having an orphan mentality and having a son or daughter mentality. The following is a summary of those key differences:

Image of God

- Orphans see God as a Master to be served. They feel as though they are constantly being watched and judged on the basis of their performance.

- Sons see God as a loving Father. He is secure in the Father's love and knows that no matter how he performs, his Father still loves him as he is.

Relationship to God

- Orphans feel like a servant or a slave. An orphan will feel they don't really deserve anything so they have to work to earn a spot in the Father's house.

- Sons feel like a son or daughter. The spirit of sonship manifests not just in how he sees the Father but in how he sees himself. He recognizes his value as a son or daughter of the King.

Approval/Affirmation

- Orphans will strive for the praise, approval, and acceptance of man. The void will have to be filled somewhere; and if it hasn't been filled with the praise, acceptance, and approval of the Father, the orphan will constantly seek it from others.

- Sons see themselves as totally accepted in God's love and justified by grace. No other praise, approval, or acceptance is necessary.

SERVICE/MINISTRY

- Orphans have a need for personal achievement. They will seek to impress God and others or will have no motive to serve at all because they feel it won't do any good anyway.

- Sons are motivated to serve out of a great love and gratitude for being unconditionally loved and accepted by God the Father.

FUTURE

- Orphans fight for everything they can get. They get bent out shape when others get something because they fear that means they won't get it.

- Sonship releases inheritance. Sons recognize everything the Father has belongs to them. They never fear lack. There is enough inheritance for all to be blessed.

SELF-IMAGE

- Orphans experience a shame-based self rejection that comes from comparing themselves with others.

- Sons feel positive and affirmed because they understand they have such a high value to their Father.

RESPONSE TO CORRECTION

- Orphans have difficulty receiving correction. They easily get their feelings hurt and close their spirit to others.

- Sons see gracious correction as a blessing and a need in their life.

SOURCE OF COMFORT

- Orphans seek comfort in counterfeit affections: addictions, compulsions, escapism, busyness, hyper-religiosity.

- Sons seek times of quietness and solitude to rest in the Father's presence and love.

PEER RELATIONSHIPS

- Orphans thrive on competition, rivalry, and jealousy toward others' success and position.

- Sons operate in humility and unity as they value others and are able to rejoice in their blessings and successes.

VIEW OF AUTHORITY

- Orphans see authority as a source of pain. They are distrustful towards authority figures and lack a heart attitude of submission.

- Sons are respectful and honoring toward authority. They see authority figures as ministers of God for good in their life.

HANDLING OTHER'S SINS

- Orphans operate in accusation and exposure in order to make themselves look good by making others look bad.

- Sons operate in love that covers a multitude of sins as they seek to restore others in a spirit of grace, truth, and gentleness.

SPIRITUAL DISCIPLINES

- Orphans practice spiritual disciplines out of duty and earning God's favor or no motivation at all.
- Sons practice spiritual disciplines out of pleasure and delight.

CONDITION

- Orphans live in bondage.
- Sons live in liberty.

SENSE OF GOD'S PRESENCE

- Orphans see God as conditional and distant.
- Sons see God as a loving Father who is close and intimate.

SECURITY

- Orphans are insecure and lack peace.
- Sons are secure and peaceful.

THEOLOGY

- Orphans live by love of the law.
- Sons live by the law of love.[1]

Satan knows if he can cause us to doubt our identity as sons and daughters of the King, that while we might be saved, he can keep us from living in power and authority as princes and princesses who advance His kingdom. He will do all he can to attack us and make us feel like orphans and not sons and daughters.

In Matthew 4 we read about Satan's temptation of Jesus. Satan attacked Jesus' identity as the Son of God.

> Then Jesus was led by the Spirit into the desert to be tempted by the devil. After fasting forty days and forty nights, he was hungry. The tempter came to him and said, "If you are the Son of God, tell these stones to become bread." Jesus answered, "It is written: 'Man does not live on bread alone, but on every word that comes from the mouth of God.'" Then the devil took him to the holy city and had him stand on the highest point of the temple. "If you are the Son of God," he said, "throw yourself down. For it is written: 'He will command his angels concerning you, and they will lift you up in their hands, so that you will not strike your foot against a stone.'" Jesus answered him, "It is also written: 'Do not put the Lord your God to the test.'" Again, the devil took him to a very high mountain and showed him all the kingdoms of the world and their splendor. "All this I will give you," he said, "if you will bow down and worship me." Jesus said to him, "Away from me, Satan! For it is written: 'Worship the Lord your God, and serve him only.'"
>
> —MATTHEW 4:1–10

I had read this passage hundreds of times and had seen very clearly how Jesus set an example of combating the enemy using the Word of God, but there was something there that I didn't notice until recently. Notice how Satan attacked Jesus in the area of sonship. In verse 3 he says, "If you are the Son of God," and again in verse 6, "If you are the Son of God." Two of the three attacks from the enemy came against Jesus' Sonship. Satan knew if he could get Jesus at the core of His identity, he would have Him right where he wanted Him.

If the enemy attacked Jesus in this area of sonship, how much more will he attack us? He will whisper in our ear and say, "You aren't worthy to be a son or daughter of the King. You know who you really are. You know what you have really done. Who do you think you are?" He knows if he can get us to think we are not sons and daughters but simply slaves who are lucky just to live in the servant's quarters, he has us right where he wants us. Satan fights every day to steal away our identity; because he knows if we get this, if we get our arms around our identity as sons and daughters of the King, we will begin to operate in the King's power and authority because we know we wear the King's name. Then and only then we will be a force to be reckoned with. So he will try everything at his disposal to trick us, scare us, and deceive us so that we lose our identity as sons and daughters of the King.

We must know who we are and whose we are. We are not servants. We are sons and daughters. We are not paupers in the kingdom. We are princes and princesses. The King has given us His name. He has included us as joint heirs with our older brother Jesus. He has given us His authority. We can do the works that Jesus did. We can have a direct personal connection with the Father by the Holy Spirit where we cry, "Abba, Daddy" (Rom. 8:15; Gal. 4:6).

There is a story about a farmer who tried to raise an eaglet among his chickens. This eaglet learned to run and scratch in the dirt. Instead of flying, he learned to look down in the dirt and run away scared of snakes. He learned to live like a chicken. But deep down in his heart, he knew something was wrong. One day he looked up and saw an eagle soaring with a snake in his talons and something resonated deep within his heart. Each time he would see an eagle soar, he knew that was his true nature. The other chickens told him to stop dreaming: "We are chickens. We are earthbound. We do not fly and we are scared of snakes." But this eagle knew who he was. He finally shook off the criticism and the earthbound mentality and soared as an eagle.

The enemy will constantly whisper in our ear that we are not sons or daughters of the King. He will try to convince us we are slaves. But the King says, "Welcome home. You are my son. You are a joint heir with your older brother Jesus and you get to soar!" Yet, a lot of us are living in an identity crisis. A lot of Christians think they are chickens when God made them to be eagles. When we were born again into the kingdom, we were given a brand-new identity. It is time that we step into it and walk in it. Everything we need to operate in the power and authority of the kingdom, to be the head and not the tail, has been given to us. The enemy would love to keep us grounded, scratching around in fear and not soaring with the eagles. He is fearful of our identity as sons and daughters of the King and will do everything he can to steal our identity. He knows the power that is available to us when we understand our true identity as children of the King.

Chapter 10

KINGDOM WARFARE

I LOVE FOOTBALL. I love the action, the hits, the competition, and the strategy. In football there is a section of the field that is referred to as the red zone. For those who might not be football fans, let me offer a quick overview. A football field is 100 yards long. It is divided into two halves by the 50-yard line that sits in the middle of the field. When the offense, the team with the ball, crosses the 50-yard line, we would say they have entered their opponent's territory. When they get to the 20-yard line, when they are 20 yards or less from getting the ball in the end zone and scoring a touchdown, that area of the field is called the red zone. So you are in the red zone when you have the ball in the last 20 yards before the end zone on your opponent's end of the field. This is really the most critical portion of the football field. Success in the game of football is often determined by how well you do in the red zone. In the red zone you are close enough to the end zone that you should put points on the board, hopefully a touchdown but at least a field goal. If you move the ball all the way down the field easily but don't get points in the red zone, you have failed. This is where the game is often won or lost. The offense steps up their game, knowing they need to score; but the defense also steps up their game in the red zone because this is the last chance to stop the offense from scoring. So the defense becomes even more aggressive, doing what they can to stop the offense from scoring.

I don't know if you've thought of it this way before, but we are living our lives in the red zone. We live deep in enemy territory and there is a lot on the line every day of our lives. You see, a lot more important than any football game is this clash of kingdoms that we find ourselves engaged in every single day of our lives. We find ourselves in the midst of a very real battle that takes place every day between the kingdom of darkness and the kingdom of light.

Ephesians 6:12 says, "For our struggle is not against flesh and blood, but against the rulers, against the authorities, against the powers of this dark world and against the spiritual forces of evil in the heavenly realms." Paul is basically saying we are living in the red zone. We are living deep in enemy territory. When we are born again, we are transferred out of the kingdom of darkness and placed into the kingdom of light. We are on a different team, but we are still living deep in enemy territory. The sad fact is that many believers are not only sitting on the sidelines watching the game but they are also oblivious to the fact that there are two opposing forces battling it out on the gridiron of life. Many believers live in complete ignorance of the enemy and the existence of the battle taking place around us all the time.

But here's the really good news: we are on the winning team!

> I saw heaven standing open and there before me was a white
> horse, whose rider is called Faithful and True. With justice he

judges and makes war. His eyes are like blazing fire, and on his head are many crowns. He has a name written on him that no one knows but he himself. He is dressed in a robe dipped in blood, and his name is the Word of God. The armies of heaven were following him, riding on white horses and dressed in fine linen, white and clean. Coming out of his mouth is a sharp sword with which to strike down the nations. "He will rule them with an iron scepter." He treads the winepress of the fury of the wrath of God Almighty. On his robe and on his thigh he has this name written: KING OF KINGS AND LORD OF LORDS. And I saw an angel standing in the sun, who cried in a loud voice to all the birds flying in midair, "Come, gather together for the great supper of God, so that you may eat the flesh of kings, generals, and the mighty, of horses and their riders, and the flesh of all people, free and slave, great and small." Then I saw the beast and the kings of the earth and their armies gathered together to wage war against the rider on the horse and his army. But the beast was captured, and with it the false prophet who had performed the miraculous signs on its behalf. With these signs he had deluded those who had received the mark of the beast and worshiped its image. The two of them were thrown alive into the fiery lake of burning sulfur. The rest were killed with the sword coming out of the mouth of the rider on the horse, and all the birds gorged themselves on their flesh.

—REVELATION 19:11–21

This is the end of the story, and it is really good news. The victory has already been won. This is a picture of the end and victory is secure, but in the meantime the battle rages.

There is another battle that is also talked about in Revelation, a battle that takes place much earlier in time. It is a battle that took place in the heavenlies as Satan, called Lucifer at this time, rose up and wanted to ascend to the throne of God. The battle raged and Satan was cast down to the earth. The dragon was enraged at the woman— the woman is Jesus. And since He couldn't defeat the woman what does He do? "Then the dragon was enraged at the woman and went off to wage war against the rest of her offspring—those who keep God's commands and hold fast their testimony of Jesus [that's us]" (Rev. 12:17).

We have been born into a world at war, and that war has been raging for thousands of years. This war isn't about high-tech fighter planes. It is not about a gladiator standing in an arena. It is not about armed soldiers storming a beach. And it's not about a war that takes place in just one part of the globe. It is a war that takes place every single day, in our backyard. It's a war that is brought to us. We are engaged in this war when we eat our dinner, when we drive to work, when we surf the Internet, when we spend our money, when we tee up on the golf course, when we worship, when we get up in the morning, when we go to bed at night, and even when we sleep. We exist in a world at war. We cannot escape this war because we are the prize. The enemy is out for our soul and the souls of our loved ones. But here's the good news: we win! We have already read the back of the book and we know we win! That means every time we engage in this battle we don't fight *for* victory, we fight *from* victory.

Ephesians 6 is one of my favorite passages of Scripture. It talks at great length about this red zone battle, deep in enemy territory, that we find ourselves in.

> Finally, be strong in the Lord and in his mighty power. Put on the full armor of God, so that you can take your stand against the devil's schemes. For our struggle is not against flesh and blood, but against the rulers, against the authorities, against the powers of this dark world and against the spiritual forces of evil in the heavenly realms.
>
> —EPHESIANS 6:10–12

The first instruction for warriors in this kingdom battle is that we must show up. Paul describes this battle as being very real. John Eldridge wrote that many of us have missed this. "It is as if we have landed on the beaches of Normandy in the early hours of D-Day, June 6, 1945, with a lawn chair and a book to read."[1] We don't engage in the battle because we don't think it is real. But the kingdom battle we find ourselves in is very real. It is not a playground. It is a battleground. Paul is clear there is a very real battle that we must show up for and be ready to engage in.

We may not be able to see it with our eyes, but it is very real. There is an intriguing story about the prophet Elisha that illustrates this well. The Israelites were at war with the King of Aram. Elisha prophesied Israel's victory, but his servant asked how he could do that since the enemy's army was so huge.

> When the servant of the man of God got up and went out early the next morning, an army with horses and chariots had surrounded the city. "Oh no, my lord! What shall we do?" the servant asked. "Don't be afraid," the prophet answered. "Those who are with us are more than those who are with them." And Elisha prayed, "Open his eyes, LORD, so that he may see." Then the LORD opened the servant's eyes, and he looked and saw the hills full of horses and chariots of fire all around Elisha.
>
> —2 KINGS 6:15–17

There was a battle raging beyond what was seen in the natural. It was just as real as the physical battle that was seen with the natural eyes that was taking place between two earthly armies. When the servant's eyes were opened, he was able to see the angel armies that were fighting on their behalf; and he then knew how the prophet was able to prophesy a victory for the Israelites.

This battle that we find ourselves in is real, but the victory is secure; yet I talk to many believers who are walking around terrified by the enemy. They are letting him kick their tail and they are doing nothing about it. They bury their head in the sand and pretend as though they are powerless to do anything about the attacks the enemy throws at them every day. In fact, based on the attitudes of many Christians I know, if I were Satan I would want them as an opponent. They walk around like a scared puppy dog with their tail tucked between their legs saying to the enemy by their passiveness and apathy, "Go ahead and trample on my life, ravage my finances, and destroy my family."

It is time we stop living in ignorance and denial. It is time to show up and fight back. We must know who we are in Christ, and, through the authority we have been given, take back ground the enemy has illegally tried to take from us.

In Samuel 17 we read about when David was a young shepherd boy, long before he was king, he went to visit his brothers at war. As he got close to the spot where the battle was raging he heard Goliath crying out, "Hey all you little wimpy Israelites. Is there no one in the land who is man enough to come out and fight me?" He was laughing and jeering at the army of Israel because no one was willing to step up and take on the fight. As David got closer and heard the cries of Goliath grow louder, he became more and more agitated. When he arrived at the Israelite camp he asked, "What's going on? What's all this noise about?" The soldiers responded, "Oh man, there's this huge giant. He is so big that no one in our camp compares to this guy. You've never seen a guy like this before, David!" David said, "Wait a second. Did you forget who you are? Did you forget whom you fight for? You are the army of the living God. Who is this guy that he would dare defy the army of the living God? I'll go fight him." David knew where his power and authority came from. He was going out to fight, not with the king's armor but with the King of king's armor. He went out to battle with a slingshot and a stone and he defeated the enemy! If this was the army of the living God and God was guaranteeing victory, then why was Goliath creating such fear in the army? Why was he taunting and terrorizing them? The only reason was because they allowed it.

George Barna reported in 2009 that only 26 percent of believers in America believe in a literal devil.[2] The vast majority of people believe he is just a sort of symbol of evil in the world. "Sort of" believing in a real enemy produces a "sort of" response that causes you to live in "sort of" defeat.

The New Testament is clear we face a real enemy. He is referred to thirty-six times as Satan, which means adversary; thirty-five times as the devil, which means slanderer; ten times as the evil one; and seven times as Beelzebub, which means lord of the flies. He is also referred to as Belial, the ruler of the prince of the air, the accuser of the brethren, the father of lies, the snake, and the dragon. That's just a sampling of titles that remind us we face a very real enemy and are engaged in a very real battle. You can dismiss him or try to ignore him, but he is referred to over 250 times, almost once a chapter, in the Word of God. It seems clear that it was in the heart of our Father to communicate the reality of our enemy.

Jesus believed the enemy was real. He encountered him head on, had conversations with demons and cast them out of people, and declared that He came to destroy the works of the devil (1 John 3:8). How long are you going to allow the enemy of your soul to taunt and terrorize you? It's time to step into the authority you have been given and say to the enemy, "Not on my watch! You won't terrorize my family. You won't plunder my health or my finances. You won't stop the church from moving forward, because Jesus said, 'I will build my church and the gates of hell will not stop it!' Satan, you don't have a gate in hell big enough or strong enough to stop the army of the living God! So we are coming after you. We are taking the battle to the streets. We aren't going to allow you taunt or terrorize or traumatize us any longer. We stand in the power of the Lord and the strength of His might."

We must remember the authority that was given to us by Jesus when He said, "I have given you authority to trample on snakes and scorpions and to overcome all the power of the enemy; nothing will harm you" (Luke 10:19). The battle is real and we must show up.

We must also power up. We must be strong as we fight this battle but not in our own strength. If we try to fight from our own strength, we will feel defeated, abandoned, let down, and blown up much of our life. Does that sound like anyone you know? Does that describe how you feel at times? If you find yourself feeling that way, it is probably because you are trying to be strong in your own strength. It is time to be strong in the Lord and in His mighty power.

The word that is translated "power" in Luke 10:19 is the Greek word *dunamis* from which we get our English word *dynamite*. It is the same power that raised Jesus from the dead. It is the same power that we receive when we are filled with the Holy Spirit. When we are strong in the Lord, we know we are on the winning side. The outcome has already been determined and our victory is sure.

When we recognize our strength comes from the Lord and the outcome is secure, we can recognize that we don't have to fight for victory because we fight from victory. We don't have to live in defeat. We don't have to feel abandoned and blown up. We don't have let the enemy eat our lunch and pop the paper bag because we are strong in the Lord.

I love the song "Great I Am." There is a part of that song that says, "The mountains shake before Him, the demons run and flee, at the mention at the name, King of Majesty!" That's more than a great line in a song. That's the truth! When we are strong in the Lord and we take His name and use His name, the enemy will have to run from us. So, "be strong in the Lord and in the power of His might" (Eph. 6:10, NKJV). The victory is ours.

Paul reminds us in the next verse to "put on the full armor of God, so you can take your stand against the devil's schemes" (v. 11). What's he saying? The enemy hasn't given up. Even though the outcome has been decided and we fight from victory and not for victory, the enemy has not pulled back his claws or tucked his tail and run away. He has schemes to take us down. If you are in Christ, he can't take your victory. He can't steal your salvation, but he will do all he can to wreak havoc in your life and keep you from living in the power and authority that belongs to you as a child of the King. So, as we live in and advance the kingdom, we need to make a decision every day to be strong in the Lord and put on our armor and show up because we live in the red zone. Our lives are still lived deep in enemy territory.

Don't be fooled into thinking you don't have to show up and armor up. Paul said the devil has schemes to try to stop you from effectively advancing the kingdom of God and you need to be aware of them. Satan hates your guts. He knows the war is over and he can't defeat you; but he will try to do the next best thing, which is to get you to live like you are defeated. "Be alert and of sober mind. Your enemy the devil prowls around like a roaring lion looking for someone to devour" (1 Pet. 5:8).

There are demons that have been assigned to attack your marriage, your kids, your finances, and your health. Anywhere that the blessing of God can touch your life, the enemy is going after that place to try to rob you of that blessing. When was the last time you considered that the opposition you are facing in your life may have satanic roots?

I'm not a guy who believes there is a demon behind every bush. It's not like I get a flat tire and think there must be a flat-tire demon out to get me; or if I burn my steak on the grill, I think that stupid bar-beque demon got me; or if I get fired it must be a bad boss demon out to get me. Maybe or maybe not. Maybe the reason for getting fired was just being lazy and not doing the job. Just a thought. But make no mistake about it, Satan and his demonic armies are on the prowl like a roaring lion seeking to devour you.

Peter wrote that the devil prowls around like a roaring lion. He doesn't say he *is* a roaring lion. He tries to imitate and intimidate, but his bark is much worse than his bite. He is *like* a roaring lion. But our King Jesus is not *like* a roaring lion, He *is* a roaring lion. He is the Lion of the tribe of Judah; and when we stand in His strength and His power and say no to the enemy in Jesus' name, we will be exercising that power and authority that is ours and we will live in the victory that has already been secured.

As warriors in this clash of kingdoms, it is important for us to realize who our enemy is. Our enemy is not our spouse, boss, drug dealers, porn distributors, Islam, Washington DC, or Hollywood, "for our struggle is not against flesh and blood, but against the rulers, against the authorities, against the powers of this dark world and against the spiritual forces of evil in the heavenly realms" (Eph. 6:12). Our enemy is Satan and his demonic forces. We must stand up and recognize with whom our real fight exists. Jesus recognized who His enemy was. He said He came to destroy the works of the devil (1 John 3:8). He went after things like sickness, disease, poverty, demonic oppression—the works of the enemy. Recognizing who the real enemy is and keeping after him is a full time job, and we won't have time to fight against others in our lives who aren't the real enemy to begin with!

We must also armor up. Paul goes on, "Therefore put on the full armor of God, so that when the day of evil comes, you may be able to stand your ground, and after you have done everything, to stand. Stand firm then, with the belt of truth buckled around your waist" (Eph. 6:13–14a). In the Roman culture the belt held the soldier's entire armor together. Every other piece of the armor was hooked to the belt. Paul said our belt is called truth. Everything else is hooked to this belt of truth. This is the first piece of armor that must be in place in our lives because Satan's number one tactic is lying. He is a liar and the father of lies (John 8:44). When he lies, he speaks his native language. English is my native language, but lying is Satan's native language. He started by lying to Adam and Eve in the Garden of Eden and he hasn't stopped ever since.

If we are going to live in the victory that Jesus has already secured for us, we must know and live in the truth. A lie doesn't have to be true to destroy us. It only has to be believed. If my wife believes I am having an affair, even if I'm not, it could destroy our marriage. Does it have to be true to destroy our marriage? No. It only has to be believed.

Satan will lie to us all the time. He will try to tell us, we are always going to be poor, or we are always going to be sick, or we are never going to amount to much. He will tell us God doesn't really love us because we are nothing more than a no-good, dirty, rotten, sinner. He will lie to keep us locked up in chains.

If we don't know the truth, we will be completely susceptible to his lies. So how do you stand in victory against his lies? You remove the lie and insert the truth. You choose to believe what God says about you whether you see it in that moment or not. We must settle in our hearts that God's Word is always true and we believe Him whether we see it at the moment or not. This is what the Bible refers to as walking by faith and not by sight (2 Cor. 5:7).

Paul instructs us in 2 Corinthians 10:5: "We demolish arguments and every pretension that sets itself up against the knowledge of God, and we take captive every thought to make it obedient to Christ." A big part of the battle we face is between our ears. We must believe the truth.

Paul mentions another part of our armor: "With the breastplate of righteousness in place" (Eph. 6:14). For the Roman soldier the breastplate was a critical piece of armor because it protected the heart and lungs. I would say that's pretty important. Our breastplate is righteousness. You may think you are not very righteous so how can you wear the breastplate of righteousness? In fact, the Bible says there is no one righteous (Rom. 3:10); but 2 Corinthians 5:21 tells us, "God made him [Jesus] who knew no sin to be sin for us, so that in him we might become the righteousness of God." The righteousness we wear is not our own. It is what theologians call imputed righteousness. It is amazing and it works like this: the moment that we trust Jesus as our Savior, all of our unrighteousness is placed upon Him and His death on the cross pays for 100 percent of it. In exchange Jesus then takes His righteousness and places it on us. We become the righteousness of Christ.

Satan will come after you and attack you with his weapons, things like guilt and shame, to keep you locked up and ineffective in the kingdom. Let me challenge you; the next time the enemy tries to do that, tell him, "I never said I was perfect but I am righteous because of Jesus. And, by the way, I memorized Romans 8:1 which tells me,

'Therefore, there is now no condemnation for those who are in Christ Jesus.'" If we can just learn the truth that in Christ we are righteous, it will transform our lives. We will start to see ourselves as God sees us. He sees us as righteous as He sees Jesus. We are able to approach the throne of grace with confidence and ask our Daddy to give us whatever we need because we are righteous in His sight. Don't miss this. We are not as good as our last day, our last decision, or our last sin. We are good as God says we are. In Christ we are righteous.

> No weapon formed against you shall prosper, And every tongue which rises against you in judgment You shall condemn. This is the heritage of the servants of the LORD, *And their righteousness is from Me*," says the LORD.
> —ISAIAH 54:17, NKJV, EMPHASIS ADDED

We must also have our "feet fitted with the readiness that comes from the gospel of peace" (Eph. 6:15). The Roman soldiers wore sandals that were strapped up to the knee and tightly fastened to their legs. The soles had nails protruding, much like modern day athletic cleats, to offer good footing. As soldiers in the kingdom we are not called to just stand and fight, we are called to advance the kingdom; and that means we must stand on good footing. The gospel, which means good news, is that good footing on which we stand. Most of the time when we think of the gospel, we think of the message of salvation. But that's an incomplete gospel message. The gospel message Jesus declared by His words and demonstrated by His works was not the gospel of salvation. It was the gospel or the good news of the kingdom, that the rule and reign of God has invaded this earth to put an end to Satan's rule and reign on the earth. As we advance the kingdom, we do so in the same way Jesus did. We are to declare the message of the kingdom and demonstrate the ministry of the kingdom.

"In addition to all this, take up the shield of faith, with which you can extinguish all the flaming arrows of the evil one" (Eph. 6:16).

Back in Paul's day, a common tactic in battle was to take an arrow, dip it in pitch, light it on fire, and shoot it at the enemy. If the arrow reached its intended target, the pain from the arrow penetrating the body and the fire burning the flesh would be intense. It would not only rip flesh on its way in, but because of the intense pain it would also cause the soldier to rip the arrow back out as fast as he could causing even more damage.

A well-placed shield could offset this enemy attack. Paul says our enemy will use not just arrows, but flaming arrows, which are designed to penetrate deep and cause us great pain. His flaming arrows are the lies and the accusations that he makes against us. He whispers in our ears things like, "You are not really loved. You are not really forgiven. You are not doing enough to earn your Father's approval. You are not giving enough." These lies are designed to bog us down with guilt.

If you ever feel accused and guilty over sin in your life, it is not from the Holy Spirit. It's from the enemy. The Holy Spirit will convict us to bring us to a point of repentance and restoration, which always brings freedom. The enemy will accuse us with fiery darts designed to inflict pain and keep us living in shame. To offset this we need the shield of faith. Faith is believing the Word of God and acting on it no matter how you feel.

"Take the helmet of salvation" (Eph. 6:17a). Obviously you can't live without your head. Goliath is the poster boy for this. Don't go to battle without your helmet on or a little boy might hit you in the head with a rock and then cut your head off! None of the rest of the armor will help at all if the helmet is not in place. If we don't have salvation, we are walking around with our head exposed and we are as good as dead.

"And the sword of the Spirit, which is the word of God" (Eph. 6:17b). This Greek word translated "word" in this passage is the word *rhema*. This is not the written Word of God. That would be the word *logos*. Rhema is the spoken word of God. This is not the Word of God on your shelf, it is not carrying the Bible in your hands, or it is not even memorizing the Word of God and simply hiding it in your heart. This is the word of God on your lips, spoken out loud. Why is this so important? Because Satan is not God, he is not omniscient. He doesn't know what we think or feel or believe in our heart. He knows what he hears; and when we declare the word of God in the name of Jesus, we will watch the enemy flee.

Notice there is no piece of armor for our back. I think that is for two reasons. The first is warriors don't turn and run. The victory is already ours so we must engage in the fight.

The second reason is that we are called to fight together. We must have each other's backs. The following is an old poem that I revised as a motto for our men's group at our church. The original author is unknown.

I Am a Warrior

I am a Warrior. I have Holy Spirit power inside of me—the same power that raised Jesus from the dead. The die has been cast. I have stepped over the line. The decision has been made. I am engaged in the battle.

I am a Warrior. I won't look back, let up, slow down, run away, or be still. I won't let the enemy ravage my marriage, my children, my finances, my health, my thoughts, or any other area of my life.

I am a Warrior. My past is redeemed, my present is powerful, and my future is secure. I am done with defeated living, sight walking, small planning, smooth knees, colorless dreams, tame visions, mundane talking, chintzy giving, and dwarfed goals. I don't have to be right, first, tops, recognized, praised, regarded, or rewarded. I now live by power, walk by faith, love by patience, lift by prayer, and labor by His might. My pace is set, my gait is fast, my goal is heaven, my road is narrow, my companions few, my Guide is reliable, and my mission is clear. I cannot be bought, compromised, deterred, lured away, turned back, diluted, or delayed. I will not flinch in the face of the attack, meander in the maze of mediocrity, hesitate in the presence of adversity, or negotiate at the table of the enemy. I won't give up, back up, let up, or shut up because I'm paid up, prayed up, armored up, and linked up with my fellow warrior to advance the cause of Christ.

I am a Warrior. I will fight until He returns, give it all until I drop, preach until all know, and never ever give up because I know I fight *from* victory, not *for* victory.

Chapter 11

KINGDOM AMBASSADORS

E VERY COUNTRY IN the world has ambassadors that represent their government in foreign lands. The United States has ambassadors in virtually every nation on earth. These ambassadors live and conduct their business in embassies. Ambassadors play an essential role by representing our nation's interests in a foreign land.

When a United States ambassador speaks, they speak with the authority of the president himself. An ambassador is authorized to act on the president's behalf. He has been delegated the authority to negotiate treaties, solicit favors, and extend either condolences or congratulations, all with the authority of the government itself.

George Shultz served as secretary of state during President Ronald Reagan's administration. I have heard that he kept a large globe in his office. When an ambassador was assigned to a particular territory and before they would actually leave, they were called into the secretary's office and he would put them to a test. He would instruct them, "I want you to go over to the globe and prove you can identify your country." Inevitably, they would go over and spin the globe and put their finger on the country to which they were being sent. That was not the answer he was looking for. He would then go on to remind his ambassadors, "Never forget you are over there in that country, but your country is the United States. You are there to represent us. Take care of our interests and never forget that you're representing the best country in the world."[1]

Being an ambassador and serving your country in a foreign land is a terrific honor, no doubt. But as Christians we have an even greater honor. We are ambassadors of Jesus Christ. When we believe in Jesus Christ and are born again into the kingdom of God, He baptizes us in the Holy Spirit to empower us to be His ambassadors. We are legal representatives of the greatest King and kingdom known to mankind: "We are therefore Christ's ambassadors, as though God were making his appeal through us. We implore you on Christ's behalf: Be reconciled to God" (2 Cor. 5:20). That is our role. We are called to be His ambassadors on this earth. God has delegated authority to us to serve as His ambassadors.

In his book *Rediscovering the Kingdom*, Myles Munroe points out that an ambassador is a unique political creature in all kingdoms and His disposition must be understood fully to understand the power and distinction of this revered position. Here are some paramount qualities of an ambassador:

- An ambassador is appointed to his position by the king. He never gets voted into the position. Our King has appointed us to serve in the role of ambassador. No one gets to vote and decide if you are qualified to be an ambassador in His kingdom.

- An ambassador is appointed to represent the state or kingdom. You represent the King's interests and have been delegated both the power and authority to advance His kingdom.

- An ambassador is committed only to the kingdom's interests.

- An ambassador embodies the kingdom.

- An ambassador is totally covered by the kingdom. All the resources, power, and authority necessary to represent the kingdom are at our disposal.

- An ambassador is the responsibility of the kingdom.

- An ambassador is totally protected by the government. The ambassador is not a member of the king's army but has full protection of the army.

- An ambassador never becomes a citizen of the state or kingdom to which he is assigned. We are residents of earth but we are citizens of heaven. Just as an ambassador of the United States remains a citizen of his country no matter what country he lives in, we are citizens of heaven, assigned to represent our King and His kingdom in this foreign territory called earth. Paul reminds us in Philippians 3 that our citizenship is in heaven. We are Christ's ambassadors, His representatives in this world. We are of little use to God if we see ourselves as anything less than citizens of heaven and ambassadors of Christ in this world.

- An ambassador can only be recalled by the king or president.

- An ambassador has access to all the king's wealth for his assignment. God has given all of His riches, the power of His Spirit, to carry out the assignment He has given to us.

- An ambassador never speaks his personal position on any issue, only what the king's official position is. Presently there are 196 countries that are recognized by the United Nations as independent sovereign nations. The United States has ambassadors in all these nations with the exception of a few where they have pulled out because of terrorist activities. Imagine if these ambassadors all decided to do their own thing. Instead of communicating with the president and speaking his position, what would happen if each ambassador did his own thing and spoke his own opinion? What if the ambassador to China spoke his own opinion and the ambassador to Germany also chose to do his own thing and they were speaking conflicting messages, neither of which were their president's position? The nation would be in huge trouble with representation like that. It is critical that every ambassador maintains a direct line of communication with the administration of the president he represents because his opinion is the only one that matters. As ambassadors of the King of kings who represent His government on earth, we are not entitled to our own opinions. We must be in constant communication with the King and speak only on His behalf and represent His interests only. Even Jesus operated this way. He said, "I only do what I see my Father doing." That is the way an ambassador functions.

- An ambassador's goal is to influence this foreign territory for his kingdom.[2]

All of these characteristics are embedded into the message and ministry of the kingdom of God, and they apply to us as ambassadors of His kingdom. We have been appointed by the King Himself to represent and advance the kingdom of heaven on earth. We are given all the rights, privileges, authority, and power that go along with that. We are ambassadors of the King of kings. We are called to voice His views and represent His heart. That's why Jesus admonished us to not worry about anything concerning our lives but instead to focus on the kingdom because then everything we need for life and fulfilling our kingdom assignment will be provided for us by the King (Matt. 6:33).

In Matthew 9 we read about Jesus sending a group out as His ambassadors to represent Him and advance His kingdom. Jesus gave them an ambassador's briefing to prepare them for their assignment. Before He sent them out as ambassadors to represent His kingdom, Jesus pulled these guys aside and told them what He wanted them to do and what they could expect as they do it. What Jesus said to this initial group of rookie ambassadors preparing for their first assignment is of great importance to each of us because we are called to be ambassadors representing His kingdom as well. Wherever you find yourself posted—your neighborhood, your workplace, or your campus—these are the instructions from the King for fulfilling the assignment He has given you as His ambassador.

What does it look like to be an ambassador advancing the kingdom?

> Jesus went through all the towns and villages, teaching in their synagogues, proclaiming the good news of the kingdom and healing every disease and sickness. When he saw the crowds, he had compassion on them, because they were harassed and helpless, like sheep without a shepherd. Then he said to his disciples, "The harvest is plentiful but the workers are few. Ask the Lord of the harvest, therefore, to send out workers into his harvest field."
> —MATTHEW 9:35–38

Jesus traveled to many places teaching the gospel of the kingdom. As He taught the message of the kingdom, He continually did the ministry that demonstrated the kingdom. He came close to people who had been oppressed by the enemy's kingdom with sickness and disease and healed them. He freed those who had been oppressed by demons. As He ministered, Jesus came across multitudes of broken and hurting people who were in need and the overwhelming needs moved His heart. Jesus knew there was a need for more people to be involved in kingdom ministry. So He turned to His disciples and instructed them to pray for the Lord of the harvest to send laborers in to the harvest field to do this kingdom work. What they didn't know in that moment was that they were part of the answer to the prayer Jesus was telling them to pray. They were praying for the Lord to send out workers, ambassadors if you will, to represent His kingdom, and He was about ready to appoint them to the post.

"Jesus called his twelve disciples to him and gave them authority to drive out impure spirits and to heal every disease and sickness" (Matt. 10:1). Jesus pulled His twelve disciples together and appointed them as the first ambassadors of his kingdom. He gave them authority to represent Him by doing what He had been doing. He assigned and empowered them to drive out evil spirits and heal all kinds of diseases. He appointed them as His ambassadors to represent both the message and ministry of His kingdom.

Before He sent them out, He gave them this ambassador's briefing. These twelve Jesus sent out with the following instructions: "Do not go among the Gentiles or enter any town of the Samaritans. Go rather to the lost sheep of Israel" (Matt. 10:5–6). This part was specific to the assignment He was sending them out on. Later He sent them to the Gentiles and Samaritans and the ends of the earth.

> As you go, proclaim this message: "The kingdom of heaven is near." Heal the sick, raise the dead, cleanse those who have leprosy, drive out demons. Freely you have received, freely give. Do not take along any gold or silver or copper in your belts—no bag

for the journey or extra shirt or sandals or a staff, for the worker is worth his keep. Whatever town or village you enter, search there for some worthy person there and stay at their house until you leave. As you enter the home, give it your greeting. If the home is deserving, let your peace rest on it; if it is not, let your peace return to you. If anyone will not welcome you or listen to your words, shake the dust off your feet. Truly I tell you, it will be more bearable for Sodom and Gomorrah on the day of judgment than for that town. I am sending you out like sheep among wolves. Therefore be as shrewd as snakes and as innocent as doves.

—MATTHEW 10:7–16

As Jesus appointed these ambassadors to go out and represent the kingdom, He gave them a message to preach—the gospel of the kingdom. We, as ambassadors of Christ, must fully understand His message and be able to communicate it in a way that speaks to a foreign culture. When an ambassador to a foreign land speaks a message, He has to translate it into the language of the people to whom He is trying to communicate. You can imagine how challenging this is. A lot of important information can be lost in the process of translation.

When Kentucky Fried Chicken translated its slogan "Finger Licking Good" into Chinese, it came out as "Eat your Fingers Off." An American T-shirt maker in Miami printed shirts for the Spanish market promoting the Pope's visit. Instead of the desired "I Saw the Pope" in Spanish, the shirts proclaimed, "I Saw the Potato."[3] A quick search of the Internet will reveal thousands of these "lost in translation" mistakes.

As ambassadors of Christ we have the responsibility of speaking clearly and accurately on behalf of Jesus Christ. We must use all means necessary to translate the gospel of the kingdom in a way that communicates clearly to the people whom we are trying to reach. The apostle Paul put it this way. "I have become all things to all people so that by all possible means I might save some" (1 Cor. 9:22). Jesus said, "As you go, preach the message of the kingdom" (Matt. 10:7).

He also instructed His followers to attach to that gospel of the kingdom a ministry that demonstrates the reality of the kingdom. What was the ministry they were to do that demonstrates the kingdom? They were told to cast out demons, heal diseases, and raise the dead. He gave them His riches, His power, and His authority to represent Him as His ambassadors.

That is the assignment He gave those first ambassadors sent to represent His kingdom and it is our assignment as well. We are to preach the good news of the kingdom. That's our message. We are to do the ministry of the kingdom—heal the sick, cleanse the lepers, cast out demons—those activities that demonstrate the reality that the kingdom of God has invaded earth. The assignment has not changed.

Jesus was very clear that this assignment of being ambassadors in His kingdom was not going to be easy. Some people will open up their homes and welcome you into their hearts and other people will slam the door and reject you.

Put yourself in the position of one of these twelve apostles. Picture yourself as the one being briefed for your assignment as a kingdom ambassador. We tend to look at the apostles and put them in stained glass and think they are larger than life, but these are ordinary guys like us. A few months earlier some of these guys had been fishermen, another was a tax collector, and all were simply ordinary, uneducated men whom Jesus had called and said, "Come, follow me" (Matt. 4:19). Now He was saying, "I don't want you to just follow, I want you to go out and represent Me. I want you to be My ambassadors and represent My kingdom by preaching the message of the kingdom and doing the works of the kingdom."

At this point, I am sure they were thinking, "What's up with that? You want us to do what? We thought we were just here to follow You, and now You want us to go and preach what You have been preaching and do what You have been doing?" Jesus said, "Yep, that's pretty much it." They probably felt a lot like you feel when you think about going out and being an ambassador of His kingdom. They probably felt unworthy. They probably weren't really sure they wanted any part of it.

That's why Jesus went on in the rest of this chapter and gave extensive instructions to help the rookie ambassadors.

> Be on your guard; you will be handed over to the local councils and flogged in the synagogues. On my account you will be brought before governors and kings as witnesses to them and to the Gentiles. But when they arrest you, do not worry about what to say or how to say it. At that time you will be given what to say, for it will not be you speaking, but the Spirit of your Father speaking through you. Brother will betray brother to death, and a father his child; children will rebel against their parents and have them put to death. You will be hated by everyone because of me, but the one who stands firm to the end will be saved.
>
> —MATTHEW 10:17–22

Jesus pointed out exactly what they could expect as ambassadors of His kingdom. You will get in trouble because you represent Me.

The same is true of us. When we go out as ambassadors representing the King of kings in our neighborhoods, workplaces, campuses, or wherever we find ourselves, there will be times we can expect to get into trouble simply because we represent Him. But Jesus also said, "Don't worry about this because you are not going out alone. You have all the resources of the kingdom at your disposal. The Holy Spirit, the very same Spirit who empowers Me to say what I say and do what I do will be in you, and in those times when you don't know what to say or do, He will tell you.

He said, "Don't be surprised when men hate you because of Me" (John 15:18–19). He was literally saying, "Don't be surprised when men hate you because of My name." Isn't it amazing how the name of Jesus is such a lightning rod? At the first inauguration of President Obama, Pastor Rick Warren was asked to pray and was instructed not to pray in Jesus' name. They told him it was okay to pray in the name of God but not Jesus. As Rick Warren wrapped up his prayer he prayed, "I humbly ask this in the name of the one who changed my life—Yeshua, 'Isa, Jesus [Spanish pronunciation], Jesus."4 He ignored the instruction because he knew as an ambassador of the kingdom he answers only to the King.

Jesus told us that as His ambassadors in a foreign land we should expect that we will face hardship because of His name. What do we do when we face this hardship? Do we stop representing and advancing the kingdom? No! Jesus said, "When you are persecuted in one place, flee to another [Matt. 10:23]. When you face persecution, don't go underground just take different ground. Don't ever stop taking ground from the enemy and advancing the kingdom."

We have been given a key mission to go out as His ambassadors to advance His kingdom. There is a kingdom that will oppose us. We can expect it but we have no reason to fear because we have been given all the resources, all the power, and all the authority of the King at our disposal. He has filled us with His Spirit so we can represent Him not just with words about the kingdom, but with works that demonstrate His kingdom as we fulfill our assignment as ambassadors.

One day Jesus asked His disciples a critical question: "Who do men say that I, the Son of man, am?" (Matt. 16:13, NKJV). They responded by saying some things like—some say you are Elijah, others John the Baptist or another prophet (v. 14). Then Jesus drew a bull's eye on them and asked pointedly, "Who do you say I am?" (v. 15). Peter piped up and replied,

> "You are the Messiah, the Son of the living God." Jesus replied, "Blessed are you, Simon son of Jonah, for this was not revealed to you by flesh and blood, but by my Father in heaven. And I tell you that you are Peter, and on this rock I will build my church, and the gates of Hades will not overcome it."
> —MATTHEW 16:16–18

Perhaps, like I did for years, you have misunderstood this verse to say that God will protect the church from the attack of the enemy.

In fact, I have heard this passage taught that way many times and it also really fit my theology pretty well too. I pictured the church in this compound, trying to survive against the big bad devil as he beat down against us. On closer examination though, that is not what this verse says. As I began to understand the kingdom, the authority and dominion that Jesus has given us to represent Him as His ambassadors and preach His message of the kingdom and do His ministry that advances His kingdom, I began to see this verse totally differently.

It does not say the armies of hell will attack the church and God will protect us. It says the gates of hell cannot prevail against the church. In other words, we are on the offensive, not the defensive. It is Satan who is cowering in fear when we advance the kingdom because he knows he doesn't have a gate big enough or strong enough to stop us when we are empowered by the King's Spirit and working as the King's ambassadors. So Jesus told us we would face trouble because of His name; but we have no need to fear, because we are ambassadors of the King of kings and nothing can stop us!

Chapter 12

ON EARTH AS IT IS IN HEAVEN

Smith Wigglesworth was quoted as saying, "If you want anything from God, you will have to pray into heaven. That is where it all is. If you live in the earthly realm and expect to receive from God, you will never get anything."[1] One of the clearest instructions we have of our assignment to pray heaven down to earth is found in what we often call the Lord's Prayer. In this prayer, Jesus told us to pray, "Your kingdom come, your will be done, on earth as it is in heaven" (Matt. 6:10).

I have often heard people pray things like, "Lord, if it is your will to heal this person of cancer..." We need to ask ourselves, "Is there cancer in heaven?" Of course there is no cancer in heaven. If there is no cancer in heaven, then we already know the Lord's will. His will is for us to pray heaven down to earth. He is clear that His will is for earth to reflect what is in heaven. That's another evidence of the assignment He has given to us in the kingdom. Many believers confuse their destiny with their assignment. Our destiny is to go to heaven someday when we die, but that is not our assignment. Our assignment is to bring heaven to earth so that His will is done on earth as it is in heaven.

Let's walk through the Lord's Prayer and see how we are to pray as we bring the kingdom of heaven to earth. This is really important for us to learn. Luke told us this prayer was given by Jesus to His disciples in response to a question. One day they came to Jesus and asked, "Lord, would You teach us to pray?" (Luke 11:1). Why did they ask that question? It is not that these disciples hadn't been taught to pray before. They were good Jewish boys, and I guarantee you they had grown up learning to pray the appropriate prayers at the set times of prayer throughout the day. So why did they want Jesus to teach them to pray? Because evidently as they had been watching Jesus for awhile and had compared their own prayer lives to Jesus' prayer life, they recognized there was something different, something distinct that took place when Jesus prayed that they didn't see when they prayed. They recognized that when Jesus prayed things happened. The sick were healed, the lame walked, the blind saw, and miracles occurred. But when they prayed, not much happened. They wondered if maybe they weren't doing it right; so they said, "Lord, would You teach us to pray?" In other words, "Jesus, we want to pray like You pray. We want to experience kingdom power when we pray the way You experience kingdom power when You pray. We want to see heaven move on earth, so Lord teach us to pray like that."

One of the things I find fascinating is that Jesus took them up on it. He said, "OK, I'll teach you to pray." The implication is that there is right way and a wrong way to pray. Before Jesus taught them how to pray in kingdom power, He first of all instructed them how not to pray.

And when you pray, do not be like the hypocrites, for they love to pray standing in the synagogues and on the street corners to be seen by others. Truly I tell you, they have received their reward in full. But when you pray, go into your room, close the door and pray to your Father, who is unseen. Then your Father, who sees what is done in secret, will reward you.

—MATTHEW 6:5–6

Religious people love to pray to impress an audience and perform for a crowd and Jesus has a name for that: hypocrite. They pray loudly and eloquently to try to impress people, but there is no power in that kind of prayer. Religious people love to put themselves out in front of people so everyone will notice them and want to be like them. While calling these hypocrites out, Jesus was saying, "Don't pray like that."

"And when you pray, do not keep on babbling like pagans, for they think they will be heard because of their many words" (v. 7). Religious people also like to heap word upon word and repeat themselves, like chanting a mantra; and Jesus said not to do that because God is a good Father and He knows what you need before you ask Him.

As a dad I would be so frustrated if my kids came up to me and said, "I want a peanut butter and jelly sandwich, I want a peanut butter and jelly sandwich, I want a peanut butter and jelly sandwich." I would say, "Look, I get it; you want a peanut butter and jelly sandwich. You don't have to ask me 100 times. I'm your dad, just ask."

Religious people don't have a good understanding of God as a loving Papa, and as a result there is not a correct understanding of prayer. Religious prayer is repugnant to God. So Jesus said don't pray like that. He said, "This, then, is how you should pray: 'Our Father in heaven...'" (Matt. 6:9). Pay attention to the fact that Jesus started with the words "our Father." At first glance we might be tempted to simply skip over this as an address kind of like "good morning" or "dear so and so" when we are writing a letter, but this is very important. God is our Father. If we really get this, if we recognize that God is our Dad and that we are His sons and daughters who are approaching a Dad who loves us very much, then we will know how to pray.

When Jesus taught His disciples to pray "our Father," it was a revolutionary concept for them. When you study the Old Testament, the word *Father* is used in reference to God only fourteen times and always refers to God as the Father of the nation of Israel. It is never used in a personal sense to refer to God as my Father personally or even as our Father collectively. There is no prayer recorded in the Old Testament in which He is referred to as Father. But Jesus taught us to pray differently, personally, to our Father.

The word translated "father" is the word *abba* which means *daddy*. This word *abba* really came to life for my wife when she visited Israel. She was walking by a school in Jerusalem and the children were outside playing when a dad came by the school. One of the children affectionately called out, "Abba!" Don't miss the significance of this. God is not impersonal. He is a very personal God. He is not some distant force out in the universe somewhere. He has a name. He is not an angry tyrant. He's a loving Dad who wants to be intimately involved in the lives of His kids. Until we grasp our identity as sons and daughters of the King, who approach Him as a Dad who is madly in love with us, we will always struggle with prayer. So Jesus said if you want to learn how to pray, don't look to religious people, look to children who have a good dad and see how they interact with their dad. That's how you learn about prayer. He moved prayer out of the realm of religious activity and put it into the context of family relationship.

"Our Father in heaven" (Matt. 6:9). Our Dad is the heavenly Creator of all things. He is the one who rules and reigns over heaven and earth. Our Dad is the King of the kingdom. He rules over all times, all places, all kings, all kingdoms, all governments, and all people. He is it. That is our Father whom we address when we pray. There is nothing and no one that is not under the authority of our Dad, so we can talk to Him about anything and He has the power and the ability to do something about it. He is sovereign. Sometimes people ask me, "If God is sovereign why should we pray?" The answer is because

God is sovereign. It's like saying my dad is in charge over everything so why should I ask him to do anything? Because he's in charge of everything! He is actually in a position to help. Because our Dad is in heaven and reigns as King over heaven and earth, He is in charge; and that should encourage us to pray with expectation.

"Hallowed be your name" (v. 9b). "Hallowed" means to be respected or revered. It is an expression of praise and worship. I believe the reason that Jesus started this prayer with worship is that worship is to be our number one priority. Psalm 22:3 says, "But you are holy, Enthroned in the praises of Israel" (NKJV). God responds to our worship by literally showing up and manifesting His presence.

Isaiah prophetically described the city of God, the place where God dwells. He wrote, "You shall call your walls Salvation and your gates Praise" (60:18, NKJV). Isaiah said the gates of God's city where we enter His presence are called praise. The gates of the city are where resources and blessings are brought in. Trade goes in and out through the city gates.

Do you get the picture? When we go through tough times and we feel defeated, when the enemy says things like, "You are bankrupt, you will never prosper," or, "you are sick and you will never be healed," we need to start praising God. God shows up and inhabits the praises of His people. Praise Him before the breakthrough is manifested. That is what the Bible calls walking by faith and not by sight. Start with praise. He is worthy. Hallowed is His name. In other words, Jesus says this Dad that we have is so good and so powerful, He's in a class all by Himself. His name is hallowed.

Names that were given to children in biblical times were often special and very meaningful, chosen sometimes to reflect something of the character of a person or some other meaning. It is kind of like when we choose nicknames to refer to someone. If we call someone slim, it's usually because they are skinny. Red means there is something red about the person, their hair color or complexion for instance. God is given many different names in the Bible. There's not always an English equivalent for the Greek or Hebrew names given for Him, so you might ask, "Which one is His real name?" The answer is, "All of them," it just depends on what mess you are in. God has a name to meet every need or every situation. While we call Him God as a generic kind of name encompassing all these things, don't forget all the other names of God. Let me give a few examples:

He is Elohim, which means Creator God. He spoke a word and out of nothing the world was created. You need to know His name Elohim because there are situations in your life where there seems to be no way out and you need a God who can create something out of nothing. When the doctors have no cure, when you have no money to pay your bills, when things are a mess and there seems to be no way out, you need you have a Daddy who is able to create something out of nothing. He can do that because that's who He is. He is Elohim.

He has another name, El Shaddai, which means the Lord Almighty. He is a Dad with incredible strength. When you are at your weakest point and find yourself exhausted with no strength left to deal with the mess you are in, God says, "You haven't exhausted all of your resources yet because I am El Shaddai. I am strong when you are weak."

He has a name El Berith, which means the God who keeps His promises. Even when the circumstances are such that it looks to you like He hasn't kept His word, He has indeed kept His word. He is a God who keeps His promises.

He is Jehovah Jirah, the God who provides. If you have a need and you don't know how to meet that need, if you need a job, if you need help out of a financial mess, you need to know who your Dad is. He is Jehovah Jirah, the God who can provide for your every need.

He is also called Jehovah Shalom, the God of peace. When things in your life are chaotic and you are stressed out, He can bring peace and calm to your soul because that's who He is, Jehovah Shalom, the God of peace.

He is Jehovah Rapha, the God who heals. The doctors may have a word but they don't have the last word. Our Dad is the Great Physician and He can heal at any time, because He is Jehovah Rapha.

Those are just some of the many names of God. You might think, "I can never remember all those names," but just remember this; He is whoever you need Him to be at the moment. When you are sick He is the doctor, when you need money He is the provider, when you need peace He is the peacemaker. You don't have to know all those Hebrew or Greek names of God you just need to ask your Dad for whatever you need and remember His name is hallowed, holy, and set apart because He has a name for any and every situation you face.

"Your kingdom come, your will be done on earth as it is in heaven" (Matt. 6:10). This verse indicates the kingdom and the will of God are tied together. It means the rule and reign of God that exists in heaven is to be brought to earth. Again, that is our assignment. The rule of God in heaven is to be mirrored on earth. The will of God in heaven is the will of God on earth. Everything that exists in heaven is to be shadowed on earth.

You may wonder, "How much of the kingdom of heaven is to be manifested here on earth? Obviously the kingdom is not here in fullness yet and there are still markings of the enemy's kingdom—things like sickness and oppression and death." I can't really answer that question, but I can tell you that when you study the way Jesus demonstrated the kingdom and the way the apostles and the early church demonstrated the kingdom, it quickly becomes obvious that much more is possible than most of us have ever experienced if we just learn to pray and bring heaven to earth.

The mandate is clear. If it exists in heaven, it is God's will for us to bring it here. Conversely, if it does not exist in heaven, our mandate is to bind it here. Jesus told us, "Whatever you bind on earth shall have been bound in heaven; and whatever you loose on earth shall have been loosed in heaven" (Matt. 18:18, NAS). Notice the phrase "shall have been." The implication is we can only bind or loose here what has already been bound or loosed in heaven. Once again heaven is our model.[2]

There are two kingdoms at war on the earth, the kingdom of darkness and the kingdom of light, the kingdom of God and the kingdom of Satan. Jesus said when you pray, remember to acknowledge that your Dad is the King of kings and that we are to declare and live in the power of His kingdom. In His kingdom, the hungry get fed, and the demonized get delivered, the sick get healed, and the poor get cared for. Because we love our Dad and are citizens of His kingdom, we want to see His kingdom show up on the earth, so we constantly pray, "Your kingdom come, Your will be done on earth as it is in heaven."

"Give us today our daily bread" (Matt. 6:11). This is praying not for spiritual but for physical needs. Is anyone hungry in heaven? Some might think prayer is all about spiritual things and they don't want to bother Dad with physical needs, but Jesus said to pray for our daily bread. We should ask for the abundant supply of heaven's resources to invade our resources. If you need a car, ask for a car. If you need a job, ask for a job. I know some people take this gospel of prosperity to an extreme and use it to fulfill greeds and not needs. But the excesses of some shouldn't keep us from claiming the promises of God for provision. Paul wrote, "My God will supply all of your needs according to His riches in glory in Christ Jesus" (Phil. 4:19, NAS). In the kingdom I am not limited to my own resources; I have all of His riches at my disposal.

"Forgive us our debts, as we also have forgiven our debtors" (Matt. 6:12). Is there any unforgiveness in heaven? Are there any grudges or bitterness in heaven? No! So again, we are called to reflect this kingdom of heaven on earth by being the most forgiving people on the planet. We all sin and we are all sinned against. When we sin we should confess our sin to God and remember we are forgiven completely because Jesus' death paid for all of our sins. When we are sinned against, we need to forgive and cancel the debt because Jesus paid our debt to God, which was far greater than the debt of sin anyone has against us. He opened a way for us to be forgiven from a mountain of sin debt we could never pay. Because of that we are called to reflect that grace to others by forgiving those who have sinned against us.

The Greek word for *forgive* means to "let it go." When we forgive someone for the wrong they do against us, we are not ignoring, accepting, excusing, overlooking, diminishing, or denying that we have been sinned against. We are not saying, "It's okay. Nobody's perfect. I understand." We aren't saying any of those things. What we are saying is, "I live in a different kingdom. I refuse to become embittered and vengeful. I will let it go because God did that for me."

"And lead us not into temptation but deliver us from the evil one" (Matt. 6:13). There is no temptation or sin in heaven, so we should pray that God's kingdom would invade our lives and protect us from the attacks of the enemy. The word *temptation* literally means "attack." Lead us not into attack. As we have already seen, spiritual warfare is real. Satan and demons are real. The kingdom of this world is filled with temptation and evil. While we can and should pray for forgiveness when we sin, we should also pray offensively in advance, before temptation comes, for protection from the evil one.

The New American Standard Bible includes a closing to this prayer which, once again, addresses the kingdom: "For Yours is the kingdom and the power and the glory forever. Amen" (v. 13, NAS). The reason we can pray for all these kingdom realities, for His will to be done on earth as in heaven, for provision of our daily bread, for forgiveness and relational healing, for protection from enemy attack, is because He is the ruler of the kingdom. The kingdom belongs to Him. The power belongs to Him. All glory all goes to Him. Jesus said this how we should pray in the kingdom.

Chapter 13

WHO IS ON THE THRONE?

O NE OF THE critical aspects to living in the power and authority of the kingdom is completely surrendering ourselves to the King. If we are saved but not living a life of intimacy with the King, if we are not fully surrendered to His rule and reign, if we are still sitting on the throne of our own heart, we will not experience the power and authority necessary to advance the kingdom, "for the kingdom of God is not a matter of talk but of power" (1 Cor. 4:20). If we are going to do more than simply talk about the kingdom, if we are going to move beyond kingdom principles to living in kingdom power, it will only come from heart fully surrendered to the King that desires an ongoing intimate relationship with Him. Even Jesus said, "I can do nothing by Myself. I can only do what I see My Father doing" (John 5:19). If Jesus could do nothing on His own but could only operate in power and authority under the direction of His Father, then we too must be fully surrendered to His agenda, His rule and reign, and His voice if we want to walk in the power and authority of the kingdom.

THE NATURAL MAN

So the question we need to ask ourselves is who is really on the throne of our lives? Paul tells us in 1 Corinthians 2:14, "But the natural man does not receive the things of the Spirit of God, for they are foolishness to him; nor can he know them, because they are spiritually discerned" (NKJV).

When we consider who is on the throne in our lives, there are three options. The first is the person who lives in Satan's kingdom under his dominion. Paul referred to that as the natural man. Understand that this is a generic use of the word *man*. He is not talking about only men. He is talking about people in general. If we were to diagram what the life of this natural man looks like, it would look something like this.

We would start with a circle and this circle represents the life of this person. In this circle there is throne. That makes sense because in every kingdom, in every life, there has to be a king. So who is sitting on the throne of the natural man's life?

"Self" is sitting on the throne of this person's life. The natural man or woman is king of their own kingdom, calling the shots in their own life.

Now let's add another element to this picture. We will add a cross representing Jesus.

When you look at the diagram, where is Jesus in the life of the natural man? This is a person who has never received Jesus into their life as Savior or Lord, so He is not even inside the circle of their life. He is on the outside looking in. So the natural man is a person who finds "self" in the center of their life. They are sitting on the throne, calling the shots as king of their own kingdom, and they have not allowed Jesus into their life at all. There is no pretense of a relationship with Him.

This is where all of us find ourselves naturally; that is why this is called the natural man. Unless or until the Holy Spirit comes upon us to draw us into a relationship with Jesus, we do not even consider spiritual things.

Inside of all of our lives there are all these different elements that comprise our personal lives. We might be in a marriage or have a family, a career, friendships, and so forth, all inside the life of this natural man.

The circles represent these different areas of relationships, interests, and activities that comprise the life of the natural man. So when it comes to this natural man, who is calling the shots in all of their relationships, interests, and activities? What's the filter through which life decisions are made? Who's sitting the throne? "Self" is sitting on the throne. Jesus is not in this person's life. He is on the outside, not involved at all, so there is really no other option through which to filter decisions than to filter them through self.

Thus when the natural man needs to make a career decision, he really has only one filter through which to process the decision: What's in it for me? How much money will I make? Will it make me happy? The same scenario is played out over and over again with every decision, relationship, or activity of this person's life. So, we would say this natural man lives a self-directed life.

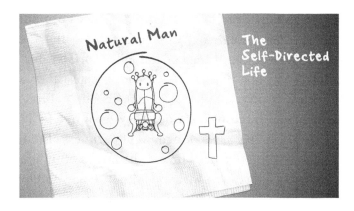

When Adam and Eve sinned in the garden and death came because of sin, what was the death that came? Obviously, we immediately think of physical death, and that would be correct; but that didn't happen immediately. But the very moment Adam and Eve sinned, their spirit died. The spirit is that part of man that was created to connect with and relate to God. That is why, unless we are born again, unless the Holy Spirit infuses our spirit and brings new life, there is no way to enter the kingdom of God because we cannot connect with and relate to Him. The natural man is born into a sinful world and he only has one birth, a physical birth. He has not experienced the second birth, being born again of the spirit. That is where every single one of us starts out. We are born as a natural person. Schools may inform us and the government may reform us but only Christ through the new birth can transform us, and this person has not yet been transformed, they have not yet been born again. This natural man may be a business person, a professor, a police officer, a banker, a good person, or a purely evil natural person, but Christ is on the outside of this person's life and there is no relationship with Him.

As we consider the kingdom, we need to ask, which kingdom is the natural man a part of? There are only two options. There are only two kingdoms are in this world. We are naturally born into the kingdom of darkness, or Satan's kingdom. The natural person is not only spiritually dead because they have not been born again, but remember what it said in 1 Corinthians 2:14 "But the natural man does not receive the things of the Spirit of God, for they are foolishness to him; *nor can he know them*, because they are spiritually discerned" (NKJV, emphasis added). In our natural state we cannot understand the things of God. They seem like foolishness to us because we are living in the kingdom of darkness. The Bible tells us that "the god of this age has blinded the minds of unbelievers" (2 Cor. 4:4), this natural man, so we cannot know God. Without a work of the Holy Spirit prompting our spirit and drawing us to God, and without ultimately that infusion of the Holy Spirit that brings about a new birth, we cannot know God and the whole God thing seems like foolishness. The idea of being a sinner and needing a Savior seems ridiculous. We think, "I'm a good person. Why do I need a Savior?" The idea of living eternally somewhere doesn't make any sense at all. The natural man, the man who has not been infused by the Spirit of God and had his spirit brought back to life through the new birth so he can connect with and relate to the things of God, will never understand the things of God. He is blind to them. They seem like foolishness to the natural man.

This is why it is absolutely foolish to witness to someone and try to tell them about the things of Christ without inviting the Holy Spirit to work on their hearts. You aren't going to simply debate or lecture someone into the kingdom of God. The only way someone's eyes can be opened and they can begin to see the things of God is by a work of the Holy Spirit on their hearts. He has to open our spiritual eyes before we can see the things of God. So it's much more important to pray than to lecture. It's much more important to invite the Spirit to open the door of someone's heart than to try to beat the door down. It doesn't work. The natural man cannot know the things of God because they are spiritually discerned.

THE SPIRITUAL MAN

But Paul doesn't stop there. He goes on: "But he who is spiritual judges all things, yet he himself is rightly judged by no one. For 'who has known the mind of the LORD that he may instruct Him?' But we have the mind of Christ" (1 Cor. 2:15–16, NKJV).

So the second type of man, or person, we see is the spiritual man.

If the natural person is someone who simply does what comes naturally, then we could say the spiritual man is a person who does what comes supernaturally. This is the person who has completely surrendered to Jesus as Savior and Lord. He has been empowered by the Holy Spirit and walks in full kingdom power because he is intimately connected with King who is calling the shots in his life.

In the life of the spiritual man, Christ is no longer on the outside of this person's life. The cross, representing Jesus, has been brought inside the circle of the spiritual man's life and is firmly planted on the throne of their life.

How did Christ get from the outside of this formerly natural man's life to the inside and make this person a spiritual person? The Spirit worked to open this person's heart to receive Christ as Savior and open their blind eyes so they could spiritually see those things that previously seemed like foolishness. When they received Jesus they were born again. That's what it means to be a Christian. Being a Christian is not about merely believing a set of beliefs or ideals. It is about receiving Someone, the person of Christ, into your heart. It's about a new life, a divine invasion into the heart of a person.

If you notice, "self" has been moved off of the throne and is at the foot of the throne yielding self's will to Christ's will.

What about those circles that represent the interests and relationships that comprise the spiritual man's life? Every career decision, every marriage decision, every parenting decision, all those day-to-day interests that drive this person's life are submitted to the lordship of Jesus Christ. They are filtered through the lens of submission to the King because He is on the throne. And notice that these circles are in order because self-will is submitted to Christ's will.

When the spiritual man was born again, they were born into the kingdom of God. So they have been transferred from the kingdom of darkness to the kingdom of light. They are living under the rule and reign of God today. They are living a life that is empowered by the Holy Spirit. They are preaching the message of the kingdom and doing the ministry of the kingdom by taking authority over the works of the enemy. They understand their role and responsibility as ambassadors working to advance His kingdom.

I would call this the Spirit-directed life. A person living a Spirit-directed life is a person that God can use to do supernatural things. In fact, a little earlier in this same chapter Paul wrote,

> "Eye has not seen, nor ear heard, Nor have entered into the heart of man The things which God has prepared for those who love Him." But God has revealed them to us through His Spirit. For the Spirit searches all things, yes, the deep things of God. For what man knows the things of a man except the spirit of the man which is in him? Even so no one knows the things of God except the Spirit of God. Now we have received, not the spirit of the world, but the Spirit who is from God, that we might know the things that have been freely given to us by God.
>
> —1 CORINTHIANS 2:9–12, NKJV

I have heard these verses used time and again by pastors to talk about heaven. It has been taught that heaven is the place that eye has not seen, ear has not heard, nor has there entered into the heart of man the things God has prepared for those who love Him. That is the context in which I have typically heard this verse quoted. While it is undoubtedly true that in heaven God has things in store for us that we have never seen or heard or can even comprehend, if you look at the context in which this is written, it is not talking about something to happen in the future. It is talking about the work of God that He wants to do through us by the power of His Spirit within the person who lives a Spirit-directed life today. This is about kingdom living. When you are born again by the Spirit of God and self is removed from the throne and Christ is given control of your life, God has miraculous things that you cannot see or imagine—incredible kingdom power and authority accompanied by signs, wonders, and miracles—for you to participate in today. Talk about having a purpose for living!

So the second type of person is the spiritual man, the person who is living a life that is totally committed to Christ, experiencing life in the kingdom.

THE CARNAL MAN

The third type of person is what I would call the carnal man.

> And I, brethren, could not speak to you as to spiritual people but as to carnal, as to babes in Christ. I fed you with milk and not with solid food; for until now you were not able to receive it, and even now you are still not able; for you are still carnal. For where there are envy, strife, and divisions among you, are you not carnal and behaving like mere men? For when one says, "I am of Paul," and another, "I am of Apollos," are you not carnal?
> —1 CORINTHIANS 3:1–4, NKJV

Paul wrote, "I would love to speak to you as spiritual people. I would love for you to be living a Spirit-directed life of kingdom power and authority." But there were people in the church in Corinth of whom he said that is not the case. They were still living off of milk, they were carnal or fleshly.

It is easy to mistake this person for the natural man. However, the carnal man is someone who has allowed Christ into their life and has been born again. Paul even refers to them as carnal Christians. They may have been saved for a while, but they are still babes in Christ. They are in Christ but He is not in control of their life. If we were to diagram this person's relationship with Christ, it might look something like this.

Again we see a circle representing their life. In this carnal Christian's life, there is also a throne and "self" is sitting on the throne. They have been born again; so unlike the natural man, Christ is on the inside of this person's life and not the outside. Now let's consider where Christ is in the carnal man's life. He is there but He has been shoved aside and is not on the throne. They have been born again but they are still living as a spiritual baby sitting on the throne of their own life and calling the shots in their own life. The carnal Christian is not living in the power of the Holy Spirit. They are not doing what they see the Father doing, they are not intimately connected in relationship to hear His voice and advance His kingdom. They are saved but living as carnal and not spiritual.

Again, the interests and relationship are there in the life of the carnal man, as they are in every one of our lives, but they are out of order. There is chaos because the carnal man is still calling the shots in their own life and not allowing the Spirit to influence their decisions and actions. They are directed by "self" because "self" is still on the throne.

Unlike the natural person, this carnal person does have Christ on the inside, and they may occasionally put Him on the throne and experience some benefits of His presence in their life; but for the most part their decisions are made pretty much made like the natural man being filtered through the lens of self.

The carnal Christian is living in the kingdom of God. They have been born again but they are not living a Spirit-directed life. In fact, we might say they are living a Spirit-neglected life.

Kingdom power and authority comes out of kingdom relationship. Kingdom power flows from not just being saved but living a Spirit-filled, Spirit-directed life. We have seen how when Jesus began His ministry He went to the Jordan River to be baptized by John and He was filled with the Holy Spirit. The Holy Spirit empowered Jesus to preach the message of the kingdom and to do the ministry of the kingdom—to heal diseases, to take authority over demons, to advance the kingdom of light in the midst of the kingdom of darkness. We have seen that when Jesus sent out the Twelve and the seventy-two they were empowered by the same Holy Spirit to go out and preach the message of the kingdom and to do the ministry of the kingdom. Following His resurrection and before His ascension, Jesus told His disciples to wait in Jerusalem for power from on high and they would become His witnesses. The Holy Spirit came on Pentecost, and by the power of the Holy Spirit they preached the message of the kingdom and they did the ministry that demonstrated the power of the kingdom. How did they do it? They did it by the power of the Holy Spirit.

Here is the point. If we want to live in power and authority and advance the kingdom; if we want to live a life of signs, wonders and miracles; it all comes by living a Spirit-directed life. If you are a believer but you are a carnal believer and self is still on the throne of your life, you might be wondering why you aren't experiencing the power and authority of the kingdom, why you aren't experiencing much joy, why it seems the enemy is wreaking havoc in your life, and you think this kingdom stuff isn't making sense at all. The reason it doesn't make sense is that even though you have the Spirit, you aren't walking by the Spirit. You are living a carnal Christian life. Self is still on the throne, and there will never be any kingdom power apart from an intimate kingdom relationship with the Holy Spirit where He is placed on the throne of your life and allowed to rule and reign.

If you are living a Spirit-neglected life, if you are saved and have been born again into the kingdom but you aren't experiencing the benefits and power of living in the kingdom, you will constantly be frustrated with the gospel of the kingdom. So ask yourself, who is on the throne of your life?

Chapter 14

NOW AND NOT YET

THERE IS THIS tension that exists when we talk about this ministry of the kingdom that cannot be ignored. While we see evidences of the kingdom of God invading earth now—as the sick are healed, demons are cast out, and even the dead are raised—we also see many evidences that the kingdom of the god of this age is still at work in this world. So the tension is this, if Jesus came to destroy the works of the enemy and put an end to His rule and reign, and if He has given us both the power and authority to continue this work in the world, then why do we still see evidence of Satan's kingdom? If Jesus came to reestablish God's kingdom on earth and to give mankind back the dominion we lost in the garden and to erase Satan's power and authority of sickness, pain, and death, then why are we still experiencing those things?

It goes back to what we said at the beginning. There is an aspect of this kingdom that is both now and not yet. Our assignment is to bring heaven to earth today, to live under the rule and reign of God today, to take authority over the works of the enemy today; but until the day King Jesus returns to rule and reign on this earth, we continue to live in the presence of the future. However, on that day we will be living in the reality of the future as the kingdom of God is fully restored on this earth and Satan's kingdom is put to an end.

While there is a right now aspect of the kingdom that Jesus not only talked about but demonstrated, and while He has delegated to us both the power and authority to continue to do the works of the kingdom, Jesus also spoke of the kingdom coming in its fullness as a future reality. He said things like, "I tell you, I will not drink from this fruit of the vine from now on until that day when I drink it new with you in my Father's kingdom" (Matt. 26:29). He is speaking of the kingdom as a future reality, or the kingdom that is not yet.

> Therefore, my brothers and sisters, make every effort to con-firm your calling and election. For if you do these things, you will never stumble, and you will receive a rich welcome into the eternal kingdom of our Lord and Savior Jesus Christ.
> —2 PETER 1:10–11

Peter is clearly speaking of the fullness of the kingdom to come that we have not yet experienced.

In Matthew 25 Jesus spoke of the Judgment Day when He said, "Then the King will say to those on his right, 'Come, you who are blessed by my Father; take your inheritance, the kingdom prepared for you since the creation of the world'" (Matt. 25:34). Obviously, this passage is speaking of the kingdom in terms of the future.

Yes, the kingdom is here now. We can live under the rule and reign of God now, but it is not here in its fullness. Don't make the mistake of leaning to either extreme. Don't take the extreme that this is the kingdom fully and this is as good as it gets. It will be so much better when King Jesus sits on the throne and reigns and the kingdoms of this earth become the kingdoms of our Lord and of his Messiah (Rev. 11:15). But also don't take the extreme that we can only wait to live in the kingdom some day and that we just have to suffer through living in Satan's kingdom today because the kingdom of God is only a future reality. That is also not true. We can live in the kingdom today. We are called to advance the kingdom today. We are to fulfill the assignment to destroy the works of the devil today. We are to call heaven to earth today. But there is this sense in which the kingdom is both now and not yet.

The kingdom of God is the rule and reign of God on this earth that Jesus came to reintroduce. It is a present reality demonstrated by the authority He took over the kingdom of Satan. He has empowered us by His Spirit to live in and operate in this kingdom now. But there is also a coming future kingdom, the millennial kingdom, when Christ will rule on this earth and the kingdom of Satan will be completely destroyed.

Many people believe this millennial kingdom is figurative and is speaking of the church age, but I believe the prophecies are clear that this is a literal rule and reign of Jesus as King of kings and Lord of lords. This kingdom in which He shall reign is not in heaven but is on earth. We are not going away to heaven, but rather heaven is coming to earth. We will go away to heaven between now and when Jesus comes back, but at the second coming the kingdom of heaven and the kingdom of earth become one. King Jesus will rule on this earth. This is not figurative but literal. The physical Jesus with a human, resurrected body, will rule and reign in bodily form on this earth.

Zechariah prophesied,

> A day of the LORD is coming, Jerusalem, when your possessions will be plundered and divided up within your very walls. I will gather all the nations to Jerusalem to fight against it; the city will be captured, the houses ransacked, and the women raped. Half of the city will go into exile, but the rest of the people will

not be taken from the city. Then the LORD will go out and fight against those nations, as he fights on a day of battle. On that day his feet will stand on the Mount of Olives, east of Jerusalem, and the Mount of Olives will be split in two from east to west, forming a great valley, with half of the mountain moving north and half moving south. You will flee by my mountain valley, for it will extend to Azel. You will flee as you fled from the earthquake in the days of Uzziah king of Judah. Then the LORD my God will come, and all the holy ones with him. On that day there will be neither sunlight nor cold, frosty darkness. It will be a unique day—a day known only to the LORD—with no distinction between day and night. When evening comes, there will be light. On that day living water will flow out from Jerusalem, half of it east to the Dead Sea and half of it west to the Mediterranean Sea, in summer and in winter. The LORD will be king over the whole earth.

—ZECHARIAH 14:1–9

Several things are prophesied here that haven't happened yet but will on the day of the Lord. The Day of the Lord was a common term in Scripture referring to the second coming of Christ. The nations have not yet been gathered to wage war against Jerusalem and the Lord has not yet taken up battle against the nations, but it will happen on that day. And Zechariah wrote that on this Day of the Lord King Jesus will set His feet on the Mount of Olives and it will be split in two. I have been to Israel twice and have stood on the Mount of Olives. It is still one mountain, but on that Day it will be split in two.

Some teach that this is figurative and not literal. But if this is figurative, why does Zechariah use specifics like the feet of Jesus and a specific mountain like the Mount of Olives? One of the rules of interpreting Scripture is: literal where possible, figurative only where necessary. I believe this is a literal promise, and it hasn't happened yet but it is going to happen because God promised it would. Zechariah also prophesied that on this Day the Lord, Messiah will rule over the whole earth. It doesn't say that He will rule over all of heaven, but rather that He will rule and reign over the whole earth. This is the millennial kingdom, and we will rule with Him in this kingdom. In Revelation 20, John describes what he saw: "I saw the thrones, and they [saints] were sat on them.... And they lived [they came alive—we are talking about the resurrection] and reigned with Jesus for thousand years" (Rev. 20:4, NKJV).

During this time of the millennial kingdom, the kingdom of God will be fully restored. The kingdom of God will be manifested in every way, affecting every single area of our lives. The evidences of Satan's kingdom, his rule and reign, will be gone; and we will live in the full effects of the kingdom restored! It will be a period of unprecedented blessing for the earth. Jesus will restore the earth to the conditions before the fall in the Garden of Eden. There will be no sickness, pain, or death. There will be no demons to battle against. There will be no mourning or sadness. Jesus will wipe every tear from our eye (Rev. 21:4).

During this millennial kingdom, Jesus will personally govern the earth as the King of all kings. He is the King of kings now, but the problem is that many kings disregard Him. There will come a day in this millennial kingdom where every knee will bow to King Jesus.

Daniel prophesied about a holy coronation of King Jesus. Daniel was writing 500 years before Christ and saw an open vision of a Jewish man being crowned King over the nations.

> As I watched, this horn was waging war against the holy people and defeating them, until the Ancient of Days came and pronounced judgment in favor of the holy people of the Most High, and the time came when they possessed the kingdom. He gave me this explanation: "The fourth beast is a fourth kingdom that will appear on earth. It will be different from all the other kingdoms and will devour the whole earth, trampling it down and crushing it. The ten horns are ten kings who will come from this kingdom. After them another king will arise, different from the earlier ones; he will subdue three kings. He will speak against

the Most High and oppress his holy people and try to change the
set times and the laws. The holy people will be delivered into his
hands for a time, times and half a time. But the court will sit,
and his power will be taken away and completely destroyed forever. Then the sovereignty, power and greatness of all the kingdoms under heaven will be handed over to the holy people of the
Most High. His kingdom will be an everlasting kingdom, and all
rulers will worship and obey him."

—DANIEL 7:21–27

The ancient of days, God Himself, gave the kingdoms of the earth
to this Man to rule and reign over the earth. This place will be perfect,
incredible, as God intended in the first place; and we will reign with
Him. It will be heaven on earth.

I heard a story about an eighty-five-year-old couple who had been
married for sixty years and were tragically killed in a car accident.
They found themselves transported outside the pearly gates where St.
Peter met them and ushered them through the gates into heaven and
began to give them a tour. He took them first to a beautiful mansion
with an incredible master suite, a Jacuzzi, and a swimming pool in
the back yard. Peter said, "This will be your home for all of eternity."
The old man asked, "How much is this going to cost?" Peter said, "You
don't get it. This is heaven. It's free."

The house bordered a beautiful golf course. Peter told them, "This
is where you will have playing privileges. Of course, every day the
course will be changed into another beautiful course so you'll never
get bored of playing at the same place." Again the old man asked,
"How much are the green fees?" Peter responded, "You don't get it.
This is heaven. It's all free. There are no tee times either. You can just
play whenever you want."

Then he took them to the clubhouse. "This is where you will eat."
It was a banquet hall filled with incredible food. The old man looked
around and said, "It looks great but where is the low fat, low cholesterol table?" Peter said, "You don't get it. This is heaven. The food is

free and you don't have to worry about things like fat grams or cholesterol. You can eat whatever you want."

At this the old man took off his cap and started stomping on it and throwing an absolute fit. Peter and his wife tried to calm him down. His wife said, "Honey, why are you so angry?" He looked at her and said, "It's all your fault. If it wasn't for those blasted bran muffins I could have been here ten years ago!"

Why is it that whenever someone tells a story about heaven and they picture it in terms of living in an incredible home or eating amazing food or having unbelievable places to play, we immediately assume we're hearing a joke? Why is it that when most of us think of an eternal kingdom we go to when we enter the afterlife we think in terms of living among the clouds, floating around aimlessly, and strumming on harps?

John Eldridge wrote, "Nearly every Christian I have spoken with has some idea that eternity is an unending church service. We have settled on this image of a never-ending sing-along in the sky, one great hymn after another, forever and ever amen. And our hearts sink. Forever and ever? That's it? That's the good news? And then we sigh and feel guilty because we're not more spiritual."[1]

Heaven is not mentioned in the Bible as existing in the clouds or the fog. The biblical picture of heaven is not some figment of our imagination. It is not a state of mind. It is a literal, physical place that is one with this earth. It is His kingdom in perfection.

> Then I saw a "new heaven and a new earth," for the first heaven and the first earth had passed away, and there was no longer any sea. I saw the Holy City, the new Jerusalem, coming down out of heaven from God, prepared as a bride beautifully dressed for her husband. And I heard a loud voice from the throne saying, "Look! God's dwelling place is now among the people, and he will dwell with them. They will be his people, and God himself will be with them and be their God.
>
> —REVELATION 21:1–3

John talked about his vision of a new heaven and a new earth. The Holy City, the New Jerusalem, comes out of heaven to earth, and earth and Heaven are brought together as one where God dwells with mankind. Think about this for a moment. Is John indicating that our ultimate destination is not in heaven somewhere but for heaven to be brought to earth and God to dwell with man? I think that's exactly what he is saying, and I think the rest of Scripture supports that idea.

Throughout Scripture the promised destination of God's people is not a non-earth where we will live in some unearthly existence up in the clouds somewhere. It is a new earth. It is a physical place. God's purpose from the beginning of time has been to live with man on a curse-free earth. In the beginning, when God created Adam and Eve and placed them in the Garden of Eden, this was how it was. God would come in the cool of the day and walk with them. But then Adam and Eve sinned. When they sinned and Satan usurped the dominion given to mankind and this earth became his kingdom, everything on earth has been different ever since. This earth is not as God originally intended it to be. Jesus came to reintroduce the kingdom and allow us to live in the kingdom of God today. It is not here in totality yet, but it will be when the kingdoms of heaven and earth become one.

The fall of man never caused God to abandon His original purpose. As you read Genesis, you will see that following Adam and Eve's sin they were removed from the Garden of Eden but Eden was never destroyed. What was destroyed by sin was man's ability to live in Eden. Man has been homesick for Eden ever since. Throughout the Bible we read prophecies that a day will come when God will make the world once again what He intended it to be in the first place. God's plan for the future is so incredible. It involves more than just redeeming mankind from sin through Jesus dying on the cross so we can have eternal life; God's plan also includes redeeming the earth from the curse it was placed under so we can experience life as God intended it to be in the first place.

It will be the ultimate restoration project. We love that concept don't we? That's why we watch those makeover shows like *Extreme*

Home Makeover or *Design on a Dime*, because we love to see the old become new. Jesus must remain in heaven "until the time comes for God to restore everything, as he promised long ago through his holy prophets" (Acts 3:21). Notice Peter said that when Jesus comes God will restore everything. He does doesn't say when Jesus comes God will destroy everything, as many of us have been taught. Peter said the Old Testament prophets talked about this renewal of all things (v. 18).

Let me give you an example:

> See, I will create new heavens and a new earth. The former things will not be remembered, nor will they come to mind. But be glad and rejoice forever in what I will create, for I will create Jerusalem to be a delight and its people a joy. I will rejoice over Jerusalem and take delight in my people; the sound of weeping and of crying will be heard in it no more.
>
> —Isaiah 65:17–19

The doctrine of the new earth where all things will be made new is talked about throughout the Bible. The prophets talked about it. The apostles taught on it. But where is this new earth that will be united with the new heaven going to be? I believe you are on it. Revelation 21:1 says there will be "a new heaven and a new earth." The word translated "new" means new in quality, not new as though it never existed. I might say to you, "Stop by and take a look at my new kitchen." It's not necessarily new in that I never had a kitchen before. It is just new because it has been restored and is now better than ever. We have never seen the earth as God made it. Our planet as we know it is only a shadowy halftone of the original. When God created the world in its original state, God said it was good (Gen 1:31). It wasn't bad until Satan and sin entered the picture.

When Jesus came, He came to reintroduce the kingdom and put an end to Satan's rule and reign on this earth. We can live in the kingdom now, but the kingdom is also not yet. When Jesus returns to rule and reign on this earth, everything under the curse will be redeemed and renewed and restored, including the earth; "no longer will there be any curse" (Rev. 22:3). The curse that God placed upon the earth when Adam and Eve sinned will be lifted. The earth will be purged and all things made new.

In this physical place, the new earth, there is a Holy City, a New Jerusalem, which comes down from heaven to earth. In Revelation 21 this city is described as a 1,500 mile cube (v. 16), meaning it goes upward too. John gave us the dimensions and those dimensions would cover some two million square miles. To try to put this in perspective, the size of this city would stretch from Canada to Mexico and from Colorado to Maine and it would be 780,000 stories high, and that's just the city. This new earth will be beyond anything we can imagine.

As we wait for the "not yet" to come, let's do all we can to live and operate in the fullness of the "now." Many use the "not yet" promises as an excuse to ignore their assignment today. It has been used to set limitations and restrictions on the kingdom power and authority we can operate in today. It has been used to ease people's dissatisfaction with a lack of kingdom power in their own lives. I have a huge problem with making the "not yet" an excuse to live with less than is available now. Our model of what is possible now is Jesus. He regularly ushered in the kingdom by taking authority over demons, healing the sick, giving sight to the blind, cleansing lepers, and even raising the dead. That's our model. We should settle for nothing less. And our assignment is clear: "Your kingdom come, your will be done, on earth as it is in heaven" (Matt. 6:10). We are not to just pray that prayer but watch it happen through our lives. Don't settle for a mediocre Christian life while you wait for what is to come in the future. There is so much more available today than most of us have dreamed or imagined as we live to fulfill our mandate to bring heaven to earth.

NOTES

CHAPTER 1
MY STORY

1.   Bruce H. Wilkinson, Paula A. Kirk, John W. Hoover, *The Daily Walk Bible* (Wheaton, IL: Tyndale House, 1997), 544.
2.   Ibid.

CHAPTER 3
RESTORING THE KINGDOM

1.   Myles Munroe, *Rediscovering the Kingdom* (Shippensburg, PA: Destiny Image, 2004), 31.
2.   George Eldon Ladd, *The Presence of the Future* (Grand Rapids: William B. Eerdmans, 1974).

CHAPTER 4
CLASH OF KINGDOMS

1.   James Strong, *Strong's Greek Dictionary of the Bible* (Miklal Software Solutions, 2011), Kindle Edition.

CHAPTER 7
BORN AGAIN INTO THE KINGDOM

1.   Munroe, 28.

CHAPTER 8
POWER SOURCE OF THE KINGDOM

1.   Jack Deere, *Surprised by the Voice of God* (Grand Rapids: Zondervan, 1996), 44.
2.   Ibid.
3.   Bill Johnson, *When Heaven Invades Earth* (Shippensburg, PA: Destiny Image, 2013), 74.

CHAPTER 9
IDENTITY CRISIS

1.   Jack Frost, *Spiritual Slavery to Spiritual Sonship* (Shippensburg, PA: Destiny Image, 2006), 120–130.

CHAPTER 10
KINGDOM WARFARE

1.   John Eldredge, "Things Are Not as They Seem," Ransomed Heart Ministries, September 2002 Newsletter, http://www.ransomedheart.com/sites/default/files/assets/newsletters/2002SepNewsletter.pdf (accessed October 23, 2013).
2.   George Barna, "Most American Christians Do Not Believe that Satan or the Holy Spirit Exist," Barna Update, April 13, 2009, https://www.barna.org/component/content/article/36-homepage-main-promo/261-most-american-christians-do-not-believe-that-satan-or-the-holy-spirit-exist#.UmgOeXBth40 (accessed October 23, 2013).

CHAPTER 11
KINGDOM AMBASSADORS

1.   George Shultz illustration found at http://www.sermonillustrator.org/illustrator/sermon4/god_tests_us.htm (accessed October 26, 2013).
2.   Munroe, 102.
3.   Translations errors found at http://termcoord.wordpress.com/2013/08/01/10-marketing-slogans-lost-in-translation/ (accessed October 26, 2013).
4.   Ted Olsen, "Rick Warren's Inaugural Invocation," *Christianity Today*, Politics Blog, January 20, 2009, http://blog.christianitytoday.com/ctpolitics/2009/01/rick_warrens_in.html (accessed October 23, 2013).

CHAPTER 12
ON EARTH AS IT IS IN HEAVEN

1.   Bill Johnson, *When Heaven Invades Earth* (Shippensburg, PA: Destiny Image, 2013), 74.
2.   Ibid., 67.

CHAPTER 14
NOW AND NOT YET

1.   John Eldredge, *Desire: The Journey We Must Take to Find the Life God Offers* (Nashville: Thomas Nelson, 2000), 111.

ABOUT THE AUTHOR

TODD HUDSON AND his wife, Tricia, together pastor Freedom Fellowship, a church plant in Highlands Ranch, Colorado that they began in 2012. They have been married for 24 years and have five children. Todd is an anointed communicator with a strong gift for teaching and preaching. He earned a Master's degree in 1991 and has been in full-time ministry for more than 25 years, leading some exciting ministries through exponential growth. Over two years ago he left a large, comfortable ministry to pursue a new movement of God after encountering the power of the Holy Spirit in his life. Todd is passionate about seeing believers realize their full potential, operating as ambassadors of the kingdom of heaven and pulling heaven down to earth.

CONTACT THE AUTHOR

Todd Hudson

todd@myfreedomfellowship.com

PO Box 631729

Highlands Ranch, CO 80163

720-663-0764

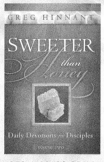

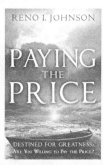
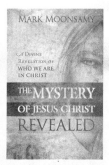